Are We There Yet?

Are We There Yet?

A Parent's Guide to Fun Family Vacations

Eileen Ogintz

HarperSanFrancisco
An Imprint of HarperCollinsPublishers

A TREE CLAUSE BOOK

HarperSanFrancisco and the author, in association with The Basic Foundation, a not-for-profit organization, will facilitate the planting of two trees for every one used in the manufacture of this book.

ARE WE THERE YET? : *A Parent's Guide to Fun Family Vacations*. Copyright © 1996 by Eileen Ogintz. All rights reserved. Printed in the United States of America. No part of this book may be used or reproduced in any manner whatsoever without written permission, except in the case of brief quotations embodied in critical articles and reviews. For information address HarperCollins Publishers, 10 East 53rd Street, New York, NY 10022.

HarperCollins Web Site: http://www.harpercollins.com
HarperCollins®, ®, HarperSanFrancisco™, and A Tree Clause Book® are trademarks of HarperCollins Publishers Inc.

Taking the Kids™ is a registered trademark of Eileen Ogintz.

FIRST EDITION

Library of Congress Cataloging-in-Publication Data:

Ogintz, Eileen.
   Are we there yet? : a parent's guide to fun family vacations / Eileen Ogintz. — 1st ed.
   ISBN 0-06-258610-6 (pbk.)
   1. Family recreation.   2. Vacations—Planning.   I. Title.
GV182.8.O336   1996   95-51276
790.1'91'—dc20

96 97 98 99 00 ❖ RRD(H) 10 9 8 7 6 5 4 3

To Andy

To Matt, Reggie, and Melanie

For the adventures we've shared and those yet to come.

Contents

Acknowledgments ix
Introduction: Thanks for the Memories xi

Part I • Ready, Set, Go

1 Vacation Countdown 3
2 Avoiding a Witch in the House 6
3 Hitting the Road 11
4 Kids on Board 16
5 Food Smarts 21
6 Education to Go 25

Part II • Stresses and Strains

7 Traveling Pregnant 35
8 Just the Three of You 40
9 Toddler Terror 45

10 Disabilities: No Barrier to Adventure   49
11 Rainy Day Blues and Other Vacation Woes   53
12 Earaches, Sniffles, and Worse   61
13 Surviving the Holiday Crush   65

Part III • Family Matters

14 Work and Play   71
15 Just the Two of Us   74
16 That First Trip as a Single Parent   78
17 It's Not the Brady Bunch   81
18 When the Kids Don't Live with You   84
19 Joining Forces   87
20 Grandma, Get Ready!   93
21 Time for Romance   97

Part IV • Vacations Everyone Will Enjoy

22 Hitting the Slopes   105
23 Beach and Water Smarts   109
24 Theme Park Etiquette   112
25 Cruise Smarts   117
26 National Parks   121
27 Kids Abroad   128
28 Pass the Culture, Please   131
29 Adventures to Go   135
30 Cows and Ducks and Horses   139

Epilogue: Happy Travels   143

Acknowledgments

If not for my family—my husband and children, my sister Amy Fieldman and her family, mom Minna Ogintz, in-laws Dominic and Lee Yemma, and the rest of the Yemma clan—neither this book nor my "Taking the Kids" newspaper column or children's books would have been written.

Thank you all for being a constant source of ideas and inspiration. Special thanks go to Matt, Reggie, and Melanie for serving, not always willingly, as my travel companions and guinea pigs and to Andy for his support and help, despite his own busy career.

I also give heartfelt thanks to the scores of parents and experts around the country, strangers and readers of my column as well as friends and neighbors, who over the past three years have gladly shared their personal "Taking the Kids" stories, disasters as well as treasured memories, along with their extensive knowledge about everything from child development to marital relations to national parks and art museums. Keep those family travel tips coming!

Last but not least, thanks to Todd Musburger for his counsel and Joann Moschella for her editor's eye.

Introduction

Thanks for the Memories

The eight-year-olds around the campfire skipped the ghost stories and songs. Instead, in the deepening Wisconsin twilight, they began telling tales of their own vacations.

It was as if the rewind button had been pushed on the VCR. The stories, accompanied by hoots and giggles, came tumbling out one after another around the glowing fire that chilly spring night: vacation disasters where everyone got sick and perfectly wonderful trips where everything went like clockwork. The kids, fingers sticky from roasted marshmallows, kept talking about visiting their cousins and grandmothers, catching bigger fish than their brothers, getting Minnie Mouse's autograph, and being dragged through "boring" museums by their parents, until the embers died and the Girl Scout leaders shepherded them into their tents and sleeping bags, everyone—including the adults—still smiling about trips long gone.

Family vacation memories do that to you no matter what your age. They are "mental movies" of each family's unique story, standing out because they're times away from frenetic daily routines and stresses. It doesn't matter how much money was spent or how exotic or mundane the locale. Vacation memories make us feel good.

Conjuring them up can sustain us in hard times. They remind us we're connected, despite thousands of miles, to those who share our history—and affection. "Souvenirs might get lost, but the kids will always have the memories," Tufts University child psychologist Don Wertlieb observes. The good times remind we adults why we're working so hard and remind the kids that we love them a lot.

Even the worst trips are funny in the retelling. A disastrous trip to Disneyland spurred a family tradition for one Oregon family. Trying to salvage something positive from the experience, the Goodmans brought home a few extra souvenirs to put in the Christmas stockings.

"That Christmas morning when the kids opened their stockings, we started laughing so hard," recalls Marsha Goodman. "We turned something that had left everyone with a bad feeling into a running family joke. We still laugh about it."

Now every Christmas the Goodman kids find their stockings stuffed with coveted souvenirs from that year's trips—a T-shirt, a tiny piece of wood from a hike in the mountains, or a snapshot of themselves at a favorite spot. Christmas morning has become a time to reminisce about happy times the family spent together.

Other families have their own terrific ideas for nurturing vacation memories. On each day of their trips, Dianne Ochiltree and her children send themselves postcards home to New Jersey, filled with what they did that day. When the family gets home, the kids put together memory books with the cards. Dianne says, "When the boys grow up, they'll each get a book of these vacation memories to take with them."

To save money on souvenirs, Debra Driscoll and family agree to buy only cloth patches from the places they visit. Once she's back home in Oregon, Debra has sewn these into quilted wall hangings for her two children's rooms.

Jill Waterman, a Los Angeles child psychologist and mother, has collages of mementos of family trips to Colorado and Hawaii hanging in her home. "Every time I walk by them, I think of those trips," she says. "It's nice to have something to help you reflect on family life." Other families cherish vacation memories of: taking the time to put vacation pictures in an album and asking the kids to write the captions; keeping vacation journals and reading them aloud to one another after getting home; handing out paper and markers on the last day and having everyone in the family draw a picture of what they liked best—and least—about the trip; and buying regional foods or a cookbook from the vacation and then using them at home for special meals, with a story-go-round about the trip at dinner.

These days, when families are stretched between jobs, sports, school, and community commitments, it's more important than ever to carve out some relaxed family time together. It doesn't need to be expensive. It doesn't need to involve complex logistics. Most important, it doesn't need to be *The Perfect Family Experience*.

That won't ever happen anyway. Besides, the kids will remember entirely different episodes than do parents. Ask my kids about Yosemite National Park and they'll laugh for twenty minutes about a game they played in the bathroom of the hotel. I remember a spectacular hike we took together to the top of a waterfall. Go figure. What matters is, we all have happy memories of that trip.

No matter how stressed or how tight the budget, squeeze in some family trips. Share adventures, telling the kids about the trips you took with your parents. Use new vacation traditions to help strengthen ties with stepparents and siblings in blended families. Bring grandparents and brothers and sisters together from around the country with their families. Take a child along on a business trip.

Wherever you go and whatever you do, remember to concentrate on each other. The museums and monuments will always be there. The kids won't. But the memories will.

Ready, Set, Go

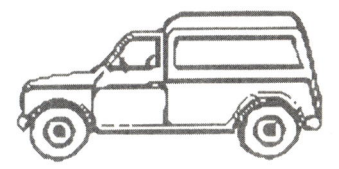

1

Vacation Countdown

Who knows what's for dinner tonight, much less what the family will want to do next August or Christmas?

Just the thought of planning a family trip months in advance can be nerve-wracking. But I'll bet you've got some ideas of things you'd like to do and can afford. Your kids will surprise you with how many ideas they've got on the subject.

So go ahead. Take advantage of winter and fall evenings to start planning. Maybe you've got to take vacation at a certain time. Maybe there's a wedding in the family that will require a trip cross-country. Maybe the airlines are offering some irresistible deals. Whatever you decide to do in the end, the time spent planning will pay off. You'll discover the kids' idea of a fun trip is a lot different from what you thought. You'll stumble on some bargains. At the very least, you won't be stuck, like one woman I know, without a hotel room anywhere in the area. "We slept in the van," she says ruefully.

These days, to get the best rates, best rooms at peak times, and best destinations, it's important to plan ahead. That's especially true for coveted resorts and national parks.

"People get so caught up in their lives they don't plan, and then they're disappointed and frustrated when they can't get what they want," says one travel agent who routinely fields requests from families that arrive too late.

So if you can, plan early! Sue Tober, a New Hampshire accountant, finalized most of her reservations for a late summer trip touring the West before Christmas—eight months before anyone in her family packed a suitcase. Families who vacation at Ludlow's Island resort in northern Minnesota routinely book for next summer before this year's vacation is done.

That's not to say you can't just get in the car and go. You can, and many families do. "That way you have to make a conscious effort to slow down," says Jill Hand, who lives in Denver. "It takes a couple of days before the kids can get into it and figure out what to do."

But planning can get both you and the kids in the spirit. You'll have fun exploring new places together before you even leave the family room. And the kids will be more involved in the trip if they've helped plan it. The anticipation will help everyone get through the dreary times and difficult tasks before vacation.

Let the kids write away for information, check out books and videos from the library, and help map the routes and choose the hotels. (Opt for swimming pools instead of atmosphere any time!) Let them investigate what kinds of things they'll want to do once they arrive. Do they want to take a hike in the mountains or go on a raft trip? Hit a certain museum or shopping mall? Is there a certain kind of food they want to try—or avoid?

Help the kids plan for their interests. Do they enjoy sports? Purchase tickets for an upcoming sports event in the area you plan to visit. Do they like exotic fish? Find an aquarium to visit. Do they get a thrill on roller-coasters? Find the biggest in the region. Are they intrigued by history? Read books or see movies set in the places you'll be visiting.

Whether it's a big trip to Europe or a simple week at the beach, advance planning can make the trip a lot smoother. Educator Lucinda Lee Katz, director of the University of Chicago Laboratory Schools, failed to plan for a sight-seeing trip to Washington, D.C., with her kids. "We spent a lot of time in the hotel calling places," she remembers. "When you've planned, you can give the children the best of activities in the area. And you're not fighting about what to do."

For kids used to having every minute taken up by school, swim practice, piano lessons, scouts, and tutoring, the prospect of a week with no set routine can be just as daunting as for parents who can't go an hour without checking their voice mail. Younger children can get even more discombobulated by shifts in their routine. "Kids' skills for using free time are primitive," suggests one child development expert. "They just don't know how to do it."

That's why no matter how laid-back the family's style, a few planned activities are always wise—just in case. No one says you've got to do them. It's vacation, after all.

To get the most bang for your vacation buck, find out when the rates change from peak to off-peak season. Sometimes, it's just a matter of adjusting a vacation schedule a few days for substantial savings and fewer crowds. Ask about packages. Many will offer a better rate for car rental, accommodations, and activities than can be had by booking directly. Inquire about family or other discounts that might apply. Hotels or attractions frequently won't advertise them but will honor them when asked.

2

Avoiding a Witch in the House

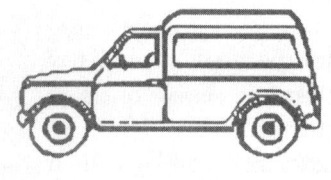

I admit it. I'm a witch before a trip. "Why are we going anyway?" I moan as I rush around frantically searching for ski mittens or bathing suits, sunscreen and toothbrushes.

Everyone has learned to stay out of my way when the suitcases come out of the closet. The night before we leave, I invariably fall into bed exhausted, convinced I've forgotten to pack the most essential items.

I never have. Besides, my husband reminds me every time, we could buy whatever we need wherever we're going. And invariably, by the time we've gotten to the airport, he and the kids are complaining that I've once again "taken too much stuff!"

So these days, I'm trying to make the packing process easier on all of us: I make the kids help and, more important, I don't leave it until the last possible moment. One frequent family traveler suggests giving each child a big box the week before the trip and letting them pick out their own clothes and toys. You simply transfer the contents of the boxes to the suitcases. That way, the kids can't complain about the clothes they've got to wear on the trip.

Jane Marcus, who lives in California, goes one step better: She hands each family member a list. They lay out their things on their beds and then their dad packs them neatly.

Joanne Cleaver, a suburban Chicago mom and travel writer, bought each of her children their own inexpensive duffel. "When they have something they want to take on the trip, they just toss it in," she says. Later, they've got room for all of their souvenirs. To help the kids stay self-sufficient on the road, some parents like to pack complete outfits together in seal-up bags or with rubber bands: shirts, shorts or pants, socks and underwear. Here's another family-tried tip: Keep a small toiletry kit packed for each child (those with hotel samples or from an overseas flight are perfect). That way nobody will forget their toothbrush. The kids I know are partial to taking their own suitcases, especially when they've got plenty of zipper compartments for secret treasures. They look at their bag as their personal space-to-go. Better to have half-empty bags, I figure, than squabbling kids arguing over their "clothes territory."

At the very least, let the kids—even preschoolers and toddlers—pack their own backpacks. They'll be proud they're old enough to help, child development experts note. Our rule: It doesn't matter what they bring, so long as they can carry the pack and have included at least one book. Of course you might want to check that your three-year-old daughter has packed something besides eight naked Barbies, as mine has on more than one occasion.

I suggest taking as many interchangeable dark-colored clothes as possible (this works great when black is hot). They may get just as dirty, but the stains will be harder to see. Throw in a couple of extra T-shirts and sweatpants. The last thing you want—as has happened to me more than once—is to find there's not a clean, dry set of clothes left. And make sure wherever you're going has laundry facilities. My favorite: a wash-and-fold place. It might cost a little more, but it's well worth the time and aggravation saved.

My kids and husband are so anxious to avoid me becoming a witch that they've become adept packers. Although the kids' duffels might not be the neatest and I still have to check to make sure they've packed pajamas and socks, it's a lot better than doing everything myself.

Learning to organize their things and pack can help older children become more independent and self-sufficient. Let each one make their own "trip list." Keep it on file on the home computer. They can adapt it as they please.

"Putting things in one place and taking them out somewhere else provides a transition," Chicago child psychologist Victoria Lavigne explains. That's especially comforting if children are going somewhere unfamiliar like camp or Dad's new home.

Be forewarned, though, that what the kids choose to put in their suitcases and backpacks won't always match your expectations. But that's fine. It's their vacation too. (Just make sure to sneak in a nice shirt or skirt for that party at Grandma's!) Any traveling parent would rather have a happy child than one grousing because he couldn't take his favorite T-shirt.

And if all this seems like a lot of trouble, think of the payoff later. When the kids are ready to pack for college, you won't have to do a thing!

Whatever you do, don't forget the toys. What do your kids like to do best—this week anyway? Play video games? Trade cards? Comb the doll's impossibly long hair? Draw pictures?

Whatever their interest or their age, there's bound to be a travel version available. These days, the travel toy industry has mushroomed to a $25 million-plus trade designed for parents desperate to amuse their pint-sized travel companions.

There are travel versions of such classic games as Scrabble, Monopoly, and Clue and art toys like Etch-a-Sketch. Racing cars and planes come in micro versions; some dolls are even smaller. And of course there are ever-growing choices for handheld video games. Some moms and many dads like to play them too.

Browse in a big toy- or bookstore several days before leaving. The idea is to have on hand some of the kids' favorites and enough new things to pique their interest when the going gets rough. Some families keep a travel bag of toys in the back of the closet and pull it out whenever a trip is in the offing. That way the toys and games all seem new.

In our house, the toys in the travel bag are regarded as old favorites, complete with warm memories of good times on past trips: Scrabble at the beach, marathon Monopoly games at the ski condo, learning to play poker at Uncle John's house.

Pack many different diversions for young children. Their attention spans are short, especially when they're confined somewhere. Older children, though, will be satisfied with one or two things they really like.

Has your preteen got a favorite music group? Present her with a new tape or CD midway through the trip to listen to on her player. Got an art lover in the house? Put together a special new "travel box" with new (washable) markers or colored pencils (fluorescents are always welcomed), stickers, scissors, stamps, and a pad of colored paper.

Throw in copies of the newest books from a favorite series or find one set in the region you're visiting. Nancy Drew mysteries, for example, are set in locales all around the country. Riddle books are always fun—especially when kids can stump Mom and Dad.

Add to the mix a destination travel book they can read, like my *Taking the Kids* series, so the backseat travelers can lead the tours. Pick up some puzzle books along the way about the places you're visiting, and bring them out when the squabbling and whining starts. The kids will enjoy them all the more after having experienced the sites.

Plastic animals also are winners. Young children and older ones alike can play with them for long stretches. Start a collection at home and let the kids add to it along the way with animals they might see: horses in Wyoming, whales in California, buffalo in South Dakota, mountain goats in Montana.

Tote things that kids can play with in different ways—toys and games that will work for one child or a group with wide age spans. You also need things that work in small spaces, like small cars and planes, finger puppets, bags of legos, or small plastic doll families with different numbers of people. Paper and markers always help. They're good for restaurants as well as planes. Ever have a tic-tac-toe tournament? Playing cards work too. Have a new card game up your sleeve to teach the gang.

Stash a couple of balls, a jump rope, bubbles and wands, pails and shovels (as good for digging in dirt as at the beach!), and, depending on the season, maybe even some roller blades, baseball mitts, and water toys. These will amuse the kids later, outdoors or in a hotel room. Vacations are a great time to wean them away from television, since programs are on different schedules in different cities.

Don't forget some amusements for Mom and Dad too. You might get a few minutes to relax—after the kids are asleep.

3

Hitting the Road

My secret weapon never fails me. On cross-country car trips that never seem to end, on harrowing drives through mountain blizzards, and during backseat battles, it magically makes tears disappear, whining quit, and grumpy faces turn into happy ones—for a moment or two anyway.

"Grab bag time!" I announce, and it's as if I've turned a knob to lower the decibel level in the backseat—and the stress quotient up front.

The kids reach into the lumpy green bag and pick out a gift-wrapped surprise. They might get glitter markers, a coveted plastic animal from the last rest stop, a book or favorite trading cards, a dress for Barbie, a comic book. (It helps to wrap each child's "picks" in the same paper.)

We're not talking anything expensive here. What counts is that whenever the going gets especially rough, the kids have

11

something to focus on besides how much longer we must drive until the hotel swimming pool.

Of course they still will ask several dozen times an hour, "How much longer?" Whether you're driving twenty miles or two thousand, the trip is too long as far as kids are concerned.

But take comfort. Millions of American parents are fighting the same backseat wars every vacation season. The Automobile Association of America reports that more than 80 percent of summer trips are taken by car. That means more than 160 million Americans are taking to the roads.

Traveling by car doesn't have to be as bad as the chicken pox. Really. There's even something positive to be said for family car trips. They're cheaper than flying. And these days, when so many families are too busy to even eat dinner together regularly, they offer the chance for family members to talk to each other.

The trick is to convince kids they're having a great time cooped up in the car, buckled into a seat belt or car seat. It's all a matter of planning with the kids in mind. Adapt to their schedules rather than yours. Eat when they regularly eat and break up the trip with frequent stops that give them the chance to burn off some energy. Adults who are driving need breaks as much as kids.

Chicago pediatrician Diane Holmes always stashes a ball in her car so her boys can play catch whenever they stop. It helps keep her energy up too.

Deb Davis, a mother of five from Genoa, Illinois, routinely forsakes restaurants for rest stop picnics. She keeps a small cooler with sandwich fixings in the trunk. "Sometimes the kids climb a tree and eat their sandwich up there. They spend most of the time running and that helps tremendously when they get back in the car. Expecting children to travel all day and behave in restaurants is too much."

A New York dad has a different solution. He routinely stops the car on long trips and makes the kids run around it seven times.

Planning some short sight-seeing stops along the way helps break up the tedium too. So do books on tape. You can borrow them from the library or many video stores these days. There's an ever-growing selection of books the entire family will enjoy. My kids sometimes ask for the same favorite story each time we take a long trip.

But when it comes to music, I draw the line. I bought each of my kids their own small tape player with earphones. It was worth every penny to avoid squabbles over who chooses the music.

Whatever you do, don't forget the snacks. If your kids are like mine, they'll announce they can't wait another minute to eat just after you've passed the last restaurant for fifty miles.

Go for things that aren't too sticky or sugary. Pretzels, raisins, crackers, fruit, string cheese, carrots, and celery are winners. Water bottles for each child are a must. They can be kept right within reach. For real emergencies, have peanut butter, jelly, and a loaf of bread on hand. But take it from one who's been there: After a few PB&J lunches on the road, you'll all be longing for anything else.

Thank goodness there's no law against driving and eating lollipops. When the kids get really antsy, hand some around. They and other treats are sure to help. For example, pass out bubble gum and stage a contest to see who can blow the biggest bubbles.

Winding roads can make even the strongest stomachs queasy—especially little ones. If car sickness becomes a problem, eat lightly and suggest the kids look out the windows, not at a book in their lap. Check with a pediatrician about motion sickness medicine if necessary.

We have some other survival goods in our stash: pine-scented cleaner and paper towels, readily accessible changes of clothes, pillows and blankets, sweatshirts and rain gear, and a cellular phone. The phone book has been a great help when we've gotten lost in unfamiliar turf.

For your safety, check the car—and the spare tire—before hitting the road. In summer, proper fluid levels are especially important. You don't want to break down somewhere at midnight. Carry a well-stocked first-aid kit, flashlight, screwdriver and pliers, and flares or reflective triangles. In winter, stocking your car with jumper cables, a small bag of sand, a shovel, and an ice scraper is a good idea too. Load luggage so it won't block the driver's view or shift during sharp turns. Carry a credit card and traveler's checks instead of a lot of cash.

---

1 🧳 *Seat Belt and Car Seat Smarts*

Car seats for small children are required in all fifty states. It's important to use them and use them correctly. Don't let anyone in your family ride—even for a few minutes—without a car seat or seat belt. Here are some seat belt and car seat tips from the National Safe Kids Campaign:

- Use a rear-facing infant or convertible seat from birth until the baby is twenty pounds. Never put a rear-facing child safety seat in the front if the passenger seat is equipped with an air bag.

- Secure the car seat in the safest place—typically the middle of the backseat. Look for a label that shows the seat meets or exceeds federal motor vehicle safety standards.

- Booster seats are for children who weigh forty to sixty pounds. Keep a child in a booster seat as long as possible.

- When using seat belts for older children, position the shoulder belt comfortably across a child's chest. It should not cut across the face or neck. Place the lap belt low and snug across the child's pelvis—below the hip bones and touching the top of the thighs. Never allow two children to share a safety belt.

Be sure to stay on well-traveled roads. Don't pick up hitchhikers, and lock the doors when you stop.

Don't forget that the whole point is to have some fun. Once the kids tire of counting license plates from different states, try singing old songs or telling funny family stories—the more embarrassing, the better.

4

Kids on Board

Face it: Airplanes just aren't made for kids. There's nowhere to run and jump. There's not enough room to spread out toys. Drinks get spilled. The air pressure hurts their ears. Other passengers get annoyed at their antics.

So what's a parent to do? Grin and make the best of it. These days you've got plenty of company. Airline officials say millions of kids are flying every year.

Whether kids fly frequently or rarely, a little planning can go a long way to ensure the trip doesn't turn into a disaster before the plane touches down. Remember, as much as the flight attendants might like kids, they can't spend time helping you take care of yours. That's your job, not theirs.

My kids—even the preschooler in the bunch—tote their own "survival packs" on board. They bring their can't-live-without possessions of the moment: neon pink markers, flaxen-haired Barbies, Nancy Drew mysteries, trading cards, and hand-held video games. Some snacks and water bottles go in the bags too, along with a clean T-shirt (in case they get sick or spill their lunch) and a sweatshirt.

I carry another "survival pack" containing an entire change of clothes for our youngest traveler, extra snacks, markers, sticker and puzzle books, a deck of cards, a wet washcloth in a plastic bag, Band-Aids, and acetaminophen (for fever or minor aches and pains). There's a chapter book to read during delays and a book for parents on the off chance that everyone falls asleep. Most important, there's a surprise present for everyone.

In our family, the "gate gift" has become a tradition. It started one vacation when I put a couple of new toys in the bag and pulled them out when we were faced with a long delay and the kids had pronounced everything they'd brought along "boring." The new inexpensive toys lightened everyone's mood immediately—even mine—and kept them amused even after we boarded. "Such good travelers," the woman in front of us said approvingly.

After that experience I might forget the tickets or the baggage claim slips, but I always remember the new toys. My kids know no matter how much they beg, they can't have them until we get to the airport gate. But that just makes it all the better. You can easily spot my kids waiting for a flight—spread out on the floor intently concentrating on their new toys. Instead of glaring, people actually smile at them. Too bad getting kids to behave isn't always that easy.

While you're waiting to board—especially with younger children—go for a walk. Kids find the hustle and bustle of airports fascinating. If the delay is long, let older kids have a scavenger hunt in the vicinity of the gate, checking off a list of things once they see them (a man with a beard; a woman carrying a briefcase; a baby in a backpack; a soldier or sailor in uniform). Make some as absurd as possible (the passenger with the most or biggest carry-on bags). Let them go buy a snack. Hand them the camera and tell them to take some goofy pictures of everyone for the vacation album.

Whenever possible, book flights around the kids' schedules—they'll be less crabby. I've got another rule: Unless there's absolutely no alternative, don't opt for the last flight of the day—it might be canceled. And even if you must pay a little more, it's always worth it to fly nonstop.

Opt for seats close to the front of the plane if you can get them, so you don't have to lug kids and backpacks to row 26. But frequently, a row or two behind the bulkhead is a better bet—because the armrests lift up and the kids can stretch out. Ask ahead if the kids might get a tour of the cockpit.

Bring gum or hard candy for older kids, in case the changing air pressure bothers them. For the same reason, plan to feed a baby when the plane takes off and lands.

Children under two may fly free, sitting on their parents' laps. But studies show that infants are far safer restrained in car seats during crashes or bumpy flights.

Parents have two choices. They may purchase a seat on the plane for the baby and bring the child's safety seat on board. (Make sure it is stamped with a label that says it is certified for use in aircraft; studies show that car booster seats are not effective.) Or they may bring the safety seat to the gate and ask the gate attendant to assign an empty seat to them. If one isn't available, the seat can be checked into baggage at the gate.

When booking the flight, inquire about children's meals. Younger kids especially like burgers or hot dogs. But remember, they must be ordered twenty-four hours in advance. If your kids are picky eaters, pack them a sack lunch to eat during the flight.

No matter what they eat, though, the younger ones will probably spill something. That's why it's wise to keep the nice outfits until you arrive at your destination. Let the kids wear their most comfortable clothes aboard the plane so you have one less thing to worry about. As for that glaring businessman across the aisle, smile sweetly and ask the ages of his kids. It might work.

If your vacation plans require your kids to fly alone, don't worry. These days, lots of kids are doing it. Some kids are barely five when they start flying by themselves. By the time they're teenagers, many kids have been winging it solo for years. And their numbers are rising—to the tune of hundreds of thousands a year. They're on almost every flight, sitting quietly by themselves near the front of the plane reading or playing with a toy. They're flying to visit Dad. They're going to Grandma's house or camp. They're even going overseas.

Some kids fly so often that they have their own frequent flier accounts. At peak summer travel times, some airlines now set aside special rooms in their terminals at hub airports where the kids may wait for flights. "Kids flying alone is a fact of life in the '90s," states one airline executive.

"I was more nervous than my son was," remarks one mother from Boston who put her eight-year-old on a flight. "He had a great time."

"We'd bring lots of stuff to do and we'd meet a lot of new people. Even grown-ups would play with us," says one young veteran flier.

No matter how often children fly alone, certain procedures must be followed. Children ages five to seven may only fly on direct flights. Children over eight may connect. Parents who want their children over twelve looked after or given help making connections must request that when they make reservations or get to the gate.

Kids flying alone pay regular adult fares, and there may be a small extra charge if they require airline assistance. You can order a child's meal at no extra cost.

Be sure to tell everyone, from the reservation agent on the phone to the gate agent to the attendant taking the tickets at the jetway, that your children are flying unaccompanied. Some airlines, like Delta or American, offer special brochures on the subject. Check with your travel agent or airline ticket office.

Get to the airport early on the big day. Make sure to bring the name, address, and phone number of the person—or people—who will be picking up your children at the other end. Also ensure that the airline has your phone number in case of an emergency. Once the kids get to their destination, a flight attendant will escort them off the aircraft into the flight arrival area. The person picking them up will need to show photo identification. That means if you've given the airline only your sister's name, your brother-in-law won't be allowed to retrieve the kids.

Here's another tip from parents of young fliers: Don't leave town yourself as soon as you've put the kids on the plane. Wait until you know the kids have arrived at their destinations. If they are going in the morning, for example, don't book yourself a flight until that afternoon or evening. It's possible that their plane will be delayed or turned back.

Be certain your children have identification and know your phone number and address—as well as those of the people who are picking them up. Do they know how to make a collect call? Do they have change for the phone? Do they have any money in case they want to buy a candy bar or a drink?

Make sure children can manage the carry-on bags themselves—and that they know they're responsible for them. The kids should be able to recognize their own suitcases. (Distinctive luggage tags will help.) Show the younger ones how to match the airline luggage stubs to those on their suitcases. Caution older ones, especially teenagers, that in case their flight is diverted, they should never leave the airport with a stranger or seek lodging themselves. Many hotels won't even accept teens without an adult. They need to know that if they're older than twelve, they must speak up and ask airline officials for help.

Now that you've taken care of everything, relax. The kids will be fine.

5

Food Smarts

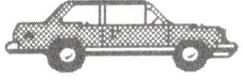

Never mind atmosphere when you're traveling with children, and skip the fancy sauces. The kids won't like them anyway.

When they're hungry, they want their food served immediately and in a fashion that's familiar. And when they're done, they want to be able to get up and leave.

Unfortunately, too many parents opt for the wrong kinds of dining places with the wrong-aged kids. That's why some talk about restaurant-going as the worst aspect of vacationing with kids.

It doesn't have to be. Stay in a condo or cabin where you can cook your own meals. Picnics are another option that is easy on the wallet—and the nerves. If you've got a kitchen, eat at least breakfast there. The kids will be happy with cereal and milk, and you'll start the day a lot quicker—with a lot less grief—than sitting through a fancy breakfast. Wait and splurge on Sunday brunch.

Certainly there's something to be said for teaching kids restaurant manners—to say please and thank you, to eat neatly and quietly with a napkin on their lap. Practice at home. Make sure to compliment them when they do well.

But don't set them up for failure. Preschoolers can't sit quietly for two hours at a stretch, and most older children won't want to either. By the same token, diners out for an adult evening will not appreciate a fidgety, whiny child at the next table.

That's why it's best to inquire ahead as to whether children are welcomed. If your children are younger or not accustomed to lengthy meals, it's always smart to choose casual restaurants over formal ones. Service will be quicker, and there probably

---

2 📖 Eating Healthy on the Road

Researchers say 25 to 40 percent of American children are overweight. At the same time, studies continue to underscore that heart disease and high cholesterol can start in childhood. Yet restaurants continue to offer high-fat fare on children's menus. Here are some strategies for everyone to eat healthier while traveling:

- When shopping in markets, pick foods that have less than three grams of fat per hundred calories.

- In restaurants, ask whether children may order half portions from the adult menu.

- Order "family style," sharing main courses rather than ordering a meal per child.

- Choose cereal rather than bacon and eggs for breakfast. Go for a walk afterward to burn up a few calories.

- Carry low-fat snacks like bagels, pretzels, carrot and celery sticks, and fruit in the car. Stay away from nuts, chips, and candy bars.

will be more things the kids will eat. You won't feel as conspicuous either or worried about how the kids are behaving. The noisier the place, the less anyone will notice them.

Arrange a sitter for your little one if you want to try that exotic spot or take the older kids out for a more formal dinner. Everyone will enjoy their evening a lot more.

This doesn't mean you're sentenced to fast-food places when traveling with the kids. Ethnic restaurants typically welcome families. Indeed, food is a natural way to help kids bridge the cultural gap, whether they're traveling across the country or the ocean. Dinner can spark a child's interest in a new place and the people who live there a lot more than many dull historic sites. Head for a teahouse serving the traditional Chinese dim sum, a barbecue pit in the Southwest, a lobster shack in Maine.

Consider limiting restaurant meals to one a day. You'll not only save money but wear and tear on your nerves. "Until kids are ten or twelve, don't expect to relax in a restaurant with them," says Chicago child psychologist Sharon Berry.

In foreign lands or even different parts of the country, let the kids shop in local markets for picnic fixings. They'll be intrigued as much with the labels and packaging as with the foods.

"Food is symbolic of how you encourage kids to open up to new experiences," explains educator Lucinda Lee Katz, director of the University of Chicago Laboratory Schools. "It gives them the message that taking a risk isn't a bad thing."

Order an unusual dish for everyone to try along with more familiar fare the kids will eat. Suggest that a new food is an adventure the family is sharing. That's not to say you should force a child to eat anything or endure a four-hour meal. Katz, for one, has eaten plenty of meals while her son has filled up on rice.

If you've got a picky eater in the bunch, it's likely worth carrying along some food from home. That's a good practice anyway for heading into restaurants when the kids are very hungry. They'll be less impatient and crabby if they can get something to eat immediately—even crackers and cheese and a juice box can make a dramatic difference.

So can something to do. Bring along a small "art box" stocked with markers, stickers and papers, a puzzle book, or a few plastic animals to keep children busy while they wait for their food. If it's appropriate, permit older children to explore outside before their food comes or after they're done eating. That's when you can sit back with that second cup of coffee.

Education to Go

The last time my husband was scheduled to attend a conference in Florida, I didn't think twice about taking the kids out of school for a few days. The chance to go with him and spend a few days together in the sun was too good to pass up.

The kids took their homework along. None of their third- or fifth-grade teachers complained. "I wish I could go," one joked.

To make sure the trip had an educational component, we also spent a day at the Kennedy Space Center. We met many families along the way.

These days, more and more parents take children out of school for vacations. Sometimes it's only during the school year that parents can get time off from work. Or traveling off-season may be the only way they can afford to go.

Pennsylvania school principal Fred Brown, who took his teenaged son out of school to accompany him to Malaysia, says, "Travel is an education."

Brown requires children to present an oral or written report on where they've been and what they've seen when they return to school. In his school, even kindergartners give "trip reports."

Wherever you go, the trip can easily become a learning experience. Have the children read about their destination or a story set there. Encourage them to keep a journal each day. They could even write on the backs of postcards they're collecting. Practice math by figuring out the cost of souvenirs or restaurant bills.

In a foreign country, there's plenty of opportunity for history, social studies, and language lessons.

Talk to the teachers beforehand about having the kids bring back souvenirs that all of the children in their class can learn from: a regional food, a game, a book. And make sure to give teachers plenty of notice to prepare any assignments that must be taken along. Another tip: Carve out the same time every day for the kids to do their homework and work on their journals, just as they would at home.

Author Laura Sutherland credits one yearlong trip in Europe when her father was on sabbatical with having lifelong benefits. "It made me confident that I could handle new situations," says Sutherland, who became an author and avid traveler. "I'm not afraid of new places." Sutherland is continuing the family tradition, taking her two grade-schoolers with her on a lengthy research trip.

To teach geography on the move, teachers urge parents to plan travel routes with the kids. Let them flex their navigational skills by guiding you from Point A to Point B. Bring along extra maps so they can follow the route along the way.

"We live in such an interdependent world, it's terribly important for children to learn about other places," says Ruth Shirey, director of the National Council for Geographic Education.

Today geography is a lot more than reading a map or being able to recite all the state capitals. It's understanding the relationship between places, people, and the environment, geographers explain. This comes at a time when Americans are woefully lacking in geography skills. Fortunately, there's a growing number of toys, books, games, and computer programs all

> ### 3 🧳 *History by Doing*
>
> The kids will never think history is boring again after a visit to one of these living history museums where actors and interpreters—including children—bring important historical periods to life. Everyone will learn something new, having fun all the while:
>
> - Plimouth Plantation, Massachusetts—the Pilgrim settlement from the 1620s (call 508-746-1622)
> - Conner Prairie, Indiana—learn about life on the plains in an 1830s pioneer village (317-776-6300)
> - Jamestown, Virginia—the first settlement in the New World, and nearby Yorktown, where the British surrendered, ending the Revolutionary War (804-229-1607)
> - Williamsburg, Virginia—an authentic Colonial city in Virginia (804-229-1000)
> - Mystic Seaport, Connecticut—tells the story of nineteenth-century shipbuilding (203-572-0711)
> - Old Sturbridge Village, Massachusetts—life in 1800s Massachusetts (508-347-3362)
> - The Henry Ford Museum, Michigan—celebrates inventors and innovators like Thomas Edison, the Wright Brothers, and Henry Ford (800-343-1929)
>
> The Smithsonian Institution's Museum of American History in Washington, though not a living history museum, is a spectacular place for a tour of popular culture. Call the Smithsonian (202-357-2700) and ask for the "Planning Your Smithsonian Visit" packet.

designed to make learning geography fun, not a chore. Two good bets for geography toys and games are the Rand McNally Catalog and the National Geography Society Catalog.

The trick to making geography attractive to kids is to keep the activities as hands-on as possible. Let the kids help decide which road to take. Can they guess how long the trip will take? Even young children can get into the act. Ask them as you travel what they see that's different from home. The desert? Mountains? Tall buildings? Talk about how the people they are meeting look different or dress differently. How is the food different from home?

See how many products the kids can name that come from the area: oranges from California, apples from Washington State, maple syrup from Vermont. Try tossing a beach ball globe around and get the kids to offer some bit of information about the place their hand touches when they catch the ball. Do map jigsaw puzzles and play geography games like "Where in the World Is Carmen Sandiego?" and "GeoSafari."

There's no better way than travel to get a good geography lesson. Just ask Jory Hecht. The California teen credited the navigating skills that helped him win the state Geography Bee to family vacations. "We always have maps all over the car," remarks his mother Ellen, a teacher.

Another way to enhance learning on the road is by visiting museums. These days every major city and many smaller ones have children's museums, or plans for one, where kids are so busy having fun making giant bubbles, trying on grown-up clothes, and using computers that they don't realize they're learning. Virtually every art museum and science center now offers hands-on areas and workshops for children and their parents, thus making science, technology, and the arts accessible to even the youngest children.

"Children grow up and if you don't get them interested in museums as children, you won't get them as adults," one museum curator explains.

"We no longer look at education as something that happens only in the classroom," says another.

The trick, museum educators acknowledge, is to make the experience fun. Museums everywhere do their part by providing plenty to engage the kids' interest—classes, one-day workshops, performances, and even special family guides to exhibitions. The Museum of Indian Arts and Culture in Santa Fe, New Mexico, for example, enables youngsters to try their hand at Native American crafts like pottery; the J. Paul Getty Museum in Santa Monica, California, offers weekend story-telling based on Greek myths.

Kids can push buttons galore in San Francisco's Exploratorium or play virtual reality basketball in Seattle's Pacific Science Center. There are now more than three hundred science centers around the country.

Wherever you're traveling, check to see what special family programs are available. Art or science museums can provide just the right antidote for bleak weather, quarreling siblings, or too many hours at the mall or with the relatives.

But don't try to see it all or spend too many hours at once. If you do, you'll get "intellectual indigestion," warns John Rhoades, director of the Bradbury Science Museum in Los Alamos, New Mexico. Instead, he suggests, concentrate on one or two exhibits.

At an art museum, ask the kids if they can imagine putting themselves inside a painting. Bring along a sketchbook for the junior artists in the family. Stop at the gift shop on the way into the art museum and buy several postcards of major artworks. Hand the kids the postcards and have a contest to see who can find each faster. It's a way to keep them looking.

If the kids are different ages or have special interests, let the family split up. Many science and art museums now have hands-on areas especially geared for preschoolers and special programming for grade-schoolers. Later, everyone in the family can compare notes on what they've seen and done.

The Association of Science-Technology Centers (202-783-7200) can tell you the location of the nearest science museum to your destination. In addition, *Doing Children's Museums* by Joann Cleaver is a good guide to the more than three hundred children's museums around the country.

Zoos and aquariums are not only fun but also ideal places to introduce children to animals, fish, and the ecosystem of the area you're visiting. Concentrate on the animals and fish that you wouldn't find at home. Talk about why they thrive in one place but not in another. Let the kids set the pace, taking time to answer their questions about each animal before moving on. The more weird facts you discover, the better.

Wherever you're traveling, you can seize the opportunity to breathe life into history. Turn a recitation of the history of the region into a tale of the children who lived there then: Atlanta during the Civil War, San Francisco during the Great Earthquake, Seattle during the Yukon Gold Rush. Look for children's books that describe the era.

Seek out living history museums or hands-on exhibitions for children at regional history museums. Kids always learn by doing. No amount of talking could match standing in a tiny Pilgrim cottage, sitting on the lumpy straw mattress, or scratching the answer to a math problem on a slate alongside a group of children dressed in Colonial garb, all of which they can do at Plimouth Plantation in Massachusetts.

At Williamsburg, Virginia, our kids drank fresh-squeezed lemonade while they listened to a guitarist sing a medley of nursery rhymes. They were astonished, and a little envious, to learn Colonial children bathed only infrequently, sleeping night after night in their underclothes.

Living history museums as well as regional museums are working harder than ever to rev up their kid appeal. Instead of a dry retelling of the historic significance of Jamestown, kids can try on soldiers' armor or maybe even help make bone tools in the adjacent Native American village. "The point is to draw the children actively into the experience," explains one Jamestown educator.

But even the best programming or the most exciting site will take a little work on parents' part. Get some books from the library before the trip, so the kids have a frame of reference once they arrive. Find a children's book set in that era or a travel book, like the *Taking the Kids* series, that will offer history in their terms. Tell them about an ancestor who might have lived through the period or your own family's history in this country.

Encourage the kids to put themselves in the place of children who might have lived in these places. What clothes would they have worn? What would they have eaten? What toys would they have had? Have them imagine life without bathrooms or VCRs. Sample some foods and buy a few historic toys to bring home.

No matter how much learning kids do on vacation, though, there will be catching up to do when they return to school. The older the children, the more they'll miss—socially as well as academically. UCLA child psychologist Jill Waterman suggests involving the children in the planning, letting them help evaluate whether the trip is worth the hassles it will cause in school.

"We'd be anxious about what we'd miss but we'd try not to dwell on it while we were there," notes Clementine Whelan, who took a trip every year with her parents and siblings that kept her out of school for a couple of weeks.

"The bad part was everything we'd miss," she says. "The good part was all of the family time when there weren't any pressures from school or friends."

II

Stresses and Strains

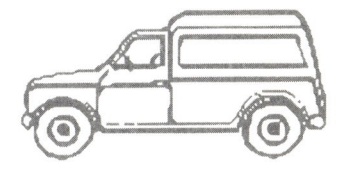

7

Traveling Pregnant

A big belly doesn't keep anyone home anymore. Pregnant women are everywhere these days: in bikinis at beach resorts, hiking in national parks, sightseeing in foreign capitals, and working in their airplane seats. Some want to squeeze in that last romantic trip before a couple becomes a threesome; many must continue to travel on business.

"You just carry on," shrugs one Los Angeles sales executive who traveled throughout her pregnancy. "I had fun wearing that bikini," laughs Dr. Eileen Murphy, a Chicago obstetrician who snorkeled every day of a Caribbean trip in her seventh month.

That's not to say it's easy or that everyone will react favorably to your presence. I found myself the recipient of many strange looks as I waddled around Paris in the seventh month of a pregnancy, ordering milk at cafes where everyone was drinking coffee and wine. On other trips, I was told by other travelers as well as waiters and hotel clerks that I should have stayed home.

It's exhausting to travel any time, but more so when you're pregnant. You may be grappling with morning sickness, swollen ankles, or sheer exhaustion. Therefore, when pregnant, plan your travel more carefully to be sure you have a comfortable room in a place where you can eat well. Consider your schedule carefully too. Rather than a hectic sight-seeing trip, perhaps opt for a beach house. Scale back the business trip or add a day so the schedule isn't packed.

"Give yourself a break and plan for down time," advises Jennifer Schade, a Chicago executive who traveled frequently on business during her first pregnancy. "You're going to need it."

Despite my best efforts, I had to curtail my pace much more than I had anticipated on my trip to Paris: I tired very easily, and it took me twice as long to shake the effects of jet lag.

---

1 📖 Pregnant Overseas

If you are going abroad or to a developing country while pregnant, the American College of Obstetricians and Gynecologists recommends the following:

- Discuss the trip with your doctor before finalizing plans. Find out where medical facilities and doctors are located in the countries you plan to visit. Register with the American embassy or consulate when you arrive. Ask for a recommendation for an English-speaking doctor.

- Drink only pure bottled water, bottled soft drinks, tea, or broth; iodine used to purify water may not be safe for pregnant women.

- Malaria, a tropical infection passed on by mosquito bites, can result in miscarriage and other problems. To avoid mosquito bites, use bug lotion and wear long-sleeved clothing. The drug chloroquine is safe to use during pregnancy and can help prevent and treat malaria.

Since you may not feel good 100 percent of the time, it's important to build some flexibility into your schedule. Don't plan to go from morning until night without a break. Do plan to give yourself enough time for leisurely and healthful meals, a period of rest during the day, and some exercise. Take a walk. Go for a swim at a nearby health club. Check out health club or pool facilities when booking hotel reservations.

Some pregnant women find they don't need to slow down at all. "Listen to your body," agrees Dr. Murphy. "Slow down when you feel you need to rest."

You don't have to prove anything to anyone when you're pregnant. During my first pregnancy, I was traveling on a newspaper assignment, and I felt great. While I was visiting a Native American reservation my hosts offered me venison sausage.

Don't travel to places that carry types of malaria resistant to that drug.

- Don't use ice in drinks or use glasses that could have been washed in impure water.
- Avoid fresh fruits and vegetables unless they've been cooked or can be peeled.
- Stay away from raw or undercooked meat. It can contain organisms that cause toxoplasmosis, a disease that could injure the baby.
- Make sure milk has been pasteurized.
- If you get diarrhea, drink plenty of fluids. Don't take any medication without checking with a doctor.
- If possible, get any necessary vaccines before getting pregnant.

I ate it, reluctant to decline their hospitality. But that night, I got sick at the airport and literally stayed sick to my stomach for the next several weeks. (It may have just been coincidence, but I'll never forget the taste of the venison.)

Acknowledge your pregnancy if you're uncomfortable eating something or taking part in some activity. And don't be afraid to ask for help or special treatment. Call hotels in advance and request a comfortable room. Ask a cab driver or an airport porter to carry your bags to the rental car van.

If you're traveling by car, pace the trip so that you're not driving more than five or six hours a day, and take frequent rest stops, doctors suggest. "Make sure you've got a comfortable car," advises Adrienne Graybrick, who lives in Des Moines, Iowa, and traveled through a twins' pregnancy. "Driving is hard on your back."

Take along a few small pillows. Tuck one behind your back and another under your feet. And don't forget to buckle your seat belt.

On planes, request an aisle seat so that you can walk around. Try to put your legs up to prevent and relieve swelling. Because the air in cabins is dry, doctors advise that you drink plenty of fluids. Carry some bottled water and eat lightly to prevent getting airsick. Pregnancy might make you more sensitive to shifts in cabin temperature, so dress in layers. If possible, avoid flying on small planes where the cabin air pressure might not be as well-regulated. Some airlines might require a doctor's note if you are flying late in your pregnancy (past six months).

Be wary of boats, especially if you haven't had much experience on board. Pregnancy is not the time for a first cruise or sailing trip. You might be even more prone to seasickness.

Being hungry at odd hours is another fact of life during pregnancy. One mom-to-be says she persuaded room service to hurry up late one night when she told them she was starved—and six months pregnant.

Although travel typically is safe at other times, the best time to travel, obstetricians say, is the fourth through sixth months. Morning sickness will be over and you'll have more energy. The rate of complications is the lowest then too.

Wherever you go far from home, take your medical records with you. Visit your doctor before you go. Ask for the name of a physician in the area you'll be visiting in case of an emergency.

Of course, traveling while pregnant has decided pluses. No one will look askance at anything you eat. People will help you with everything from directions to carrying your luggage. You can gracefully exit a boring late business dinner.

And you don't have to worry about how you look in a bathing suit.

8

Just the Three of You

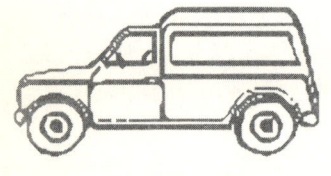

The Caribbean setting was perfect, complete with blue seas and moonlit nights. The baby couldn't have been more miserable. She got sick. Her nap schedule made sight-seeing forays impossible. She didn't want to eat. She was covered with so many mosquito bites she looked like she had the chicken pox.

Her parents, who have always loved to travel, couldn't wait for the trip to be over. "If the baby was unhappy, I was unhappy," remembers Julie Faude, a Philadelphia psychologist. "It was very exhausting and stressful."

Ask parents about their first vacation with the baby and they'll likely talk about it the way a soldier recalls boot camp: It had its moments, but it wasn't an experience they want to repeat. "Save your money till they're older," sighs one California child psychologist who remembers a particularly horrendous trip when her boys were babies.

But traveling with a baby isn't doomed to be a disaster as long as parents know going in that the trip will be nothing like their holidays as a couple.

Cindy Yingling recalls a trip to Florida with her infant. She returned so pale that colleagues said they were sorry the weather had been so bad. But the sun had shined plenty. She just hadn't had time to get out and enjoy it. "I understand now what it means to go on vacation with a baby," she says. "You don't get any *you* time." Her advice: Think of it as a change of scene, not a vacation.

Another new mom remembers going away with her mother-in-law, thinking Grandma would be delighted to baby-sit. "But Grandma didn't want to baby-sit at all," she remarks ruefully. "She wanted us to entertain her."

Her advice: Plan ahead for time away from baby. You'll need it. If grandparents are in the picture, make sure they're willing to baby-sit. Otherwise, arrange for a sitter. Ask friends or colleagues who live in the area and have young children to suggest one. Ask hotel officials who have young children to recommend their favorite sitters. Frequently, hotel employees will take the job themselves.

But remember that everyone won't think your baby is as adorable as you do. Before heading to a swank restaurant, consider whether the other patrons will be giving you dagger eyes the entire meal. Many people go to restaurants to get away from their kids. If the baby starts screaming in a public place, get up and leave.

Pediatricians caution new parents to think hard about their travel destination when they've got an infant in tow. Young babies can get very sick very quickly, spiking high fevers or suffering from dehydration. You won't want to be hours from first-rate medical care. Consider opting for Florida instead of a tiny Caribbean island; Paris rather than a remote French village; your parents' house instead of that cabin in the mountains.

You must remember some other cautions when traveling with infants. For example, although babies' skin is especially sensitive to sun, pediatricians don't recommend using sunscreen for those under six months old. Plant a wide-brimmed sun hat on their heads, a tightly weaved cotton shirt over their tummy, and park them in the shade, under a beach umbrella. Give them plenty to drink to be sure they don't get dehydrated.

Never leave home without buckling the baby securely in a car seat. If you must feed your baby, either stop or sit next to the infant. Here's a tip for keeping the baby amused en route: Tape bright, colorful pictures of babies in the car for the baby to look at.

A word about planes: Infants may be more sensitive to the changes in air pressure than you are. Sucking helps tremendously to alleviate pressure, so as the plane takes off and lands, nurse the baby or offer a bottle or pacifier.

Forget traveling light. There's the car seat, stroller, diaper bag, port-a-crib, and toys, just to name a few essentials. A baby backpack or front carrier for infants are great for sight-seeing too.

"I used to be the guy who would grab my carry-on bags, jump off a plane and into a cab," says Joe Clark glumly from his southern California home. "Now it's three suitcases, two carry-ons, and a diaper bag, and you're constantly overtipping because you're so guilty asking people to help you schlep."

Don't forget an assortment of toys—new ones and old favorites. Board books are always good bets. So are keys and mirrors and stacking cups. Wherever they are, babies crave the familiar comforts of home. Savvy parents say something as simple as bringing along an infant's own crib sheet, night-light, and tape player with a favorite tape for use at Grandma's or at a hotel makes all the difference between a fussy and a content child. The same goes for car seats. Babies will like the familiar feel of their own seat. Most important: Remember that special "lovey."

You also want to be sure the place you're going not only is baby-friendly but also has everything you'll need: a crib, a refrigerator, elevators, baby-sitters. Hint: Most places that have baby supplies are likely to welcome families with young children. A hotel or guest house that can't provide a crib probably doesn't want your business. This might be the time to consider a suite hotel or a condo rather than that quaint inn. I remember spending five days with all of us in one room. It was impossible for the baby to nap—or for us to relax, for fear of waking her.

Nap schedules probably have wrecked more new parents' vacations than bad weather, flight delays, or misplaced hotel reservations. The baby's time clock won't adjust as quickly as yours. I recall one trip to the West Coast when we arrived in the middle of the night: Because of the time change, the baby thought it was morning and was busy playing at 4 A.M.

2 📁 Travel Survival Pack for Babies—and Their Parents

Keep these stashed within easy reach or in a carry-on bag on a plane:

- At least two complete changes of clothes for the baby, including an extra sweatshirt or jacket
- More diapers, wipes, formula, and food than you expect to need—in case of delays. A bottle of water also is a good bet
- Favorite "lovey"
- New toys: a plastic mirror, keys, and board books all are good items to have on hand when immediate diversion is needed
- Collapsible stroller
- A clean shirt for Mom or Dad

But it won't be all bad, and new parents hitting the road with an infant as soon as possible will find it easier to adjust to the change in traveling styles.

There's another reason parents find it easy to adjust to traveling with an infant: Tiny babies can be easy traveling companions. They don't take up much room. They stay where you put them. They can't race away to wreak havoc with anything in their path. If you're nursing, they don't even need much food.

Maybe you won't have many leisurely dinners on moonlit terraces this trip, but the baby's smiles will make up for it—hopefully, anyway.

9

Toddler Terror

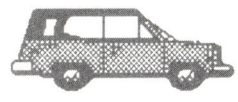

Three-year-old Melanie wouldn't budge until she'd drawn a giant M in the sand. It took several tries before she was satisfied.

She refused to be rushed anywhere along that rocky Oregon beach. She wanted to investigate every grain of sand, turn over every stone, touch every slimy sea creature she could find. Her older brother and sister, exasperated, ran ahead down the beach.

Melanie wanted her shirt on—and then off. She wanted to be carried, but then she wanted to run. She was always either hungry or thirsty, cold or hot.

That's traveling with a three-year-old: always frustrating, never predictable. Forget the schedule. Melanie was always hungry after everyone had finished eating and wide awake when the rest of the family was ready to drop into bed. We couldn't take our eyes off of her for an instant because she'd race away.

But having Melanie along on that trip and many others added a dimension that I wouldn't have missed for anything.

Her sense of wonder about new places and new things made us all stop to look.

"A crab!" she said triumphantly as she peered into a tidepool. When the older kids looked where she was pointing, they found all kinds of tiny ocean creatures they would otherwise have missed.

She made us laugh and strangers smile. Some struck up conversations with us, offering advice about where to go or what to see.

We were more relaxed because we'd given up trying to keep to a rigid schedule.

The trick to traveling with toddlers and preschoolers, I decided, was to slow down and look at the world from their viewpoint rather than expecting them to see places through adult eyes.

"We went berry-picking instead of antiquing," says Nancy Hammond, who lives along the Oregon coast and took her preschooler to visit Grandma on the East Coast. "We walked around Grandma's neighborhood a lot."

"We don't go to countries where the main activities are fine dining and art museums," shares a Chicago mother who has traveled widely with her preschoolers. "Forget those romantic dinners for two. It's not going to happen."

Figure that nothing will go as planned with a toddler along. The Chicago mother also recalled the time her husband left her and her daughter in a cab reading a story while he went sightseeing.

Don't head off to a beach resort, ski area, or cruise ship thinking your toddler will be thrilled to spend all day in a children's program full of strangers. Be prepared that he or she may not.

But young kids might be more adaptable than you might think. It helps if they can stick fairly closely to their regular meal and sleep times. If they still nap, make sure they get a break. If they eat peanut butter every day for lunch, make sure you've got some on hand (along with bread). If they want the same story read every night, make sure you've brought it along.

Remember, with little kids, it's the seemingly inconsequential things that can make all the difference between a wonderful trip—and one that's a disaster. No three-year-old, for example, can wait until 8 P.M. for dinner or skip lunch in favor of an art exhibit.

If possible, child development experts suggest, plan your trip so that there will be other kids the same ages around, as well as other adults. You might even be able to get a break by trading off child-care responsibilities for a couple of hours now and then.

Even better, let the kids have a say in where you're going that day. A museum to see dinosaurs or a playground? Try to schedule plenty of "play time" every day.

Give toddlers ample time to adjust too: Time and weather changes affect kids just like they affect you. Rather than plunging into a frenetic pace, take it slow the first few days. Encourage them to try new things, but don't force it. That's just asking for trouble.

Little ones might want to ride the same attraction at a theme park six times instead of hitting all the different ones or stay in the same small area of a museum. Let them; they feel more secure that way. When they're tired and cranky, it's time to leave. (But try telling a three-year-old that it's time to go because *Mom's* cranky.)

Another thing to remember when traveling with toddlers is to use the same vigilance about accident prevention as you do at home. One day Melanie managed to get into the glove compartment of our minivan, open a child-proof lid on a bottle of Dramamine, and guzzle the entire thing—all within about two minutes—while we were unloading the car. She and I spent the night in the hospital, where she was hooked up to all kinds of monitors as she slept off the overdose. Luckily, she was fine the next day.

Doctors warn that whenever people make changes from their usual routines, the likelihood of accidental injury increases. Some hotels now offer parents a safety kit. When you book, ask whether child-proofed rooms are available.

Always keep your eyes on children around water. If gates surround a pool, make sure they are kept closed and locked. Always buckle kids in life jackets when in a boat. Check carefully for windows without screens or guards (all too easy for a toddler to tumble out) and balconies with too-wide slats in the railings.

10

Disabilities: No Barrier to Adventure

Ten-year-old Allison Jones raced down the Colorado mountain, her long hair flying. Skiing on one leg didn't slow her down a bit.

"She skis better than I do," says her mother Diane proudly. "I'm always asking her to slow down."

These days, kids with disabilities are rafting down rivers, touring foreign capitals, rock climbing up mountains, and hitting Hawaiian beaches.

"That's how you learn about life . . . having adventures," says Vicky Bishop, whose fourteen-year-old son Jeremy is wheelchair bound as a result of spina bifida.

It used to be that most families whose children were disabled simply didn't venture far from home. Travel was too difficult. Wheelchairs wouldn't fit in hotel bathrooms. High curbs made city strolls frustrating. Restaurants didn't want to serve them. There were stares and uncomfortable questions.

But then came the 1990 Americans With Disabilities Act (ADA), which mandated accessibility. Ever since, a generation of determined parents are taking to the road, carrying wheelchairs, crutches, and medicines as they camp, ski, and visit resorts.

The ADA has enabled the growing numbers of families rearing children with disabilities to normalize their family life. Much more adaptive equipment is available to do everything from skiing to mountain biking to touring the country by van.

At the same time, families with children who have disabilities have discerned a decided change of attitude in society: The public is far more welcoming to them than in the past. Parents of physically or mentally challenged children urge people not to just stare or stay away. Ask questions, and the families will be glad to answer.

It's a win-win situation. The children with disabilities are able to enjoy a far broader range of activities and places, and other children gain a far more realistic view of those with disabilities by seeing them in action. The message children receive is: Kids with disabilities are able and active, just like me.

Sports especially are a huge confidence builder for children with disabilities or chronic illness as well as for their parents. "When you see a child with disabilities doing something their siblings can do, your spirit soars," says Hal O'Leary who, in his position as founder and director of the National Sports Center for the Disabled at Winter Park, Colorado, has watched parents see their children skiing for the first time. "You realize there's a future for that child."

That optimism and self-confidence carry over to other parts of the child's life, fostering success in school and a higher sense of self-esteem. "I feel so free on the mountain," grinned Jeremy Bishop after he first skied down it in a special "sit-ski."

Families of disabled kids or those with chronic illness can continue to enjoy the activities they have always shared, exploring new places together. Hundreds of outdoor recreation activities are now available for these children and their families. Many national parks also offer at least one trail accessible to those with disabilities, with accessibility improving all the time.

"People are more than willing to accommodate you if you explain what you need," notes one California mother, adding that her son, now in his twenties, has become such a good traveler he now goes on his own.

Before heading out, check with a local children's or rehabilitation hospital in the area you'll be visiting to find out about special programs. Probably they could even recommend sitters for a child with special needs, or doctors should the child need one. Ask about accessible playgrounds or nature trails.

Check with hotels or campgrounds to be certain your family can be accommodated comfortably. Even Disney World now provides a special guide for disabled guests.

3 Winter Park

The National Sports Center for the Disabled in Winter Park, Colorado, which started as a one-time effort to help a group of pediatric amputees from Denver enjoy the winter, has become the world's model program to teach disabled adults and children how to ski in winter and enjoy the mountains in summer. Adaptive equipment for forty-five disabilities is even provided at a large workshop.

In summer the center offers wheelchair-accessible camping, mountain biking, and rock climbing for the blind. Families come from around the world to enjoy the facilities (call 303-726-5514).

For those who prefer less-organized forays into the wilderness, there's the excellent *Easy Access to National Parks* from the Sierra Club.

This is not to say there aren't still barriers. There are, and they can be exceedingly frustrating. Airline bathrooms, for example, can be very tricky, parents note. That's why it's important to do your homework before heading out, asking lots of questions. And be prepared for foul-ups.

I recall one very distraught woman who arrived at a national park lodge—reservations made months before—who wasn't given a wheelchair- accessible room, though she'd requested one. After much wrangling and apologies, adjustments were made.

"Sure everything is harder," says Gail Flannagan, whose daughter Colleen has served as a youth spokesperson for the Easter Seal Society. "It's still worth doing. Focus on what they can do, not on their weakness."

11

Rainy Day Blues and Other Vacation Woes

I'd come ready for the beach, stuffing the suitcases with everything from sunscreen to sunglasses, pails and shovels, Frisbees, and even an inflatable turtle inner tube for our preschooler. It hadn't occurred to me it might rain.

But that's what we got in Florida—for four solid days. To my surprise, we all had a good time anyway, and I learned a valuable lesson: Just because plans go awry doesn't mean a vacation is ruined.

Of course you'll be disappointed and even frustrated. But if you're able to shift gears to accommodate the weather or a sprained ankle—or whatever catastrophe has befallen you that day—you can still have a good time.

Martha Melvoin, for one, says her two California-raised boys love the rain at their grandparents' Maine cottage because it is so decidedly different from home. "They get on their slickers and go out and fish," she says.

Unfortunately, when it comes to vacations, too many of us have a hard time accepting anything different from what we'd planned. We've got an indelible mental image of what the trip is supposed to be: perfection. We're certainly paying enough for the privilege, and we badly need the family time together. No wonder with all that self-induced pressure, stress has become the dirty little secret of family travel.

"I get grumpy as soon as we pull out of the driveway," says Kevin Leonard, a Chicago librarian. "Everything falls apart when you go on vacation," he sighs. "It's probably better to stay home and do the laundry."

Not likely. But traveling with kids won't ever be ideal. And the vacation will be just like the kids—noisy, messy, and irritating, with enough glimmers of wonderful to remind you why you took them in the first place.

Lower your expectations and you'll ease your stress quotient considerably—no matter what the weather. Deborah Lerner Duane says her secret is a siesta every afternoon on vacation.

California author Carole Meyers recalls one rainy trip to Hawaii when the weather wreaked havoc with her family's plans. But the kids spent much of their time building houses out of cards in the hotel lobby, attracting a whole audience and thoroughly enjoying themselves. "I keep a pack of cards in my suitcase at all times," laughs Meyers, who has written widely about family travel.

Board games can work wonders to chase away the rainy day blues. If you're going to have access to a VCR, stash a few favorite tapes in the suitcase for those "when all else fails" times.

Planning activities with the kids in mind will help too. They won't want to spend three hours eating dinner in a fine restaurant or touring one art exhibit. Opt for a more casual meal and a quicker museum tour.

Mark Ludlow, a Minnesota resort owner and father of four, suggests that rainy days are ideal for visiting a local factory or a fire station. His kids have seen pineapple processed in Hawaii, beer brewed in Colorado, and potato chips fried in Minnesota.

"It's the parents who mind the rain, not the kids," laughs Ludlow.

Instead of getting upset, consider some glitch in the vacation schedule as a chance to really kick back. Sleep late. Linger over breakfast. Read a chapter book to the kids by the fire. If you've got access to a kitchen, spend the afternoon baking cookies. If you don't, head to a shopping mall—while your husband and kids watch a movie. Sometimes giving yourself a break is the best stress buster of all.

Remember that vacations are stressful for kids too—strange beds, no friends, no video games or refrigerators. It's wise to plan less rather than more. If their idea of fun is splashing in the indoor pool or watching a movie in the room, let them. It's their vacation too.

Vacations are times when daily routines are neglected. You might skip breakfast or naps, stay up late, or eat an extra ration of treats. And that can be enough to exacerbate sibling battles—even in places the kids want to go. That's why experts say it's important to impose some routine and sense of discipline on the road. Be forewarned that younger children are especially sensitive to changes in routines—meal- and bedtimes, for example—and may react by snatching a toy from their baby sister or bopping a brother on the head.

You can separate siblings, threaten them, or punish them. You can try to use psychology. But they are still going to fight.

"Kids may fight more on vacation if they are together more than they are at home," notes UCLA child psychologist Jill Waterman, herself the veteran of many backseat skirmishes between her twin sons. "Wherever you go on vacation, your family dynamics go with you."

Of course, what you want on vacation is a respite from all the bickering, punching, and teasing that goes on at home from breakfast until bedtime. You especially wish for that in public places like restaurants, hotel lobbies, and theme park lines. Unfortunately, the fact that strangers are watching isn't usually enough to quiet the warring factions. Remember that kids like to fight.

Don't just ignore the situation. Respond as you would at home. In a public place, experts suggest, give the kids a warning—and a choice. "We can stay or we can leave and not have dessert . . . buy that souvenir . . . play that arcade game . . . " One suburban Chicago mother of three will take away swimming privileges for an afternoon or television for an evening. The important thing is to follow through after a warning.

---

4 *Sight-seeing Survival Guide*

Lace up those broken-in tennis shoes. Grab the map and the guidebook. Don't forget the camcorder. It's time to take the kids to see the sights. Sure you can sightsee with the kids in tow, as long as you remember the rules. They'll keep the kids happy—and you sane.

RULE 1: Forget long bus tours (unless you've got an infant who will nap anywhere), and give up on the idea of following a guide through a museum or historic site, unless you've somehow stumbled on a tour that's meant for families.

RULE 2: Spend some time at home reading up with the kids about where you're going and what you'll be seeing from a child's perspective. The more comfortable they are in a new environment, the better traveling companions they'll make.

RULE 3: Tell the kids what they'll be seeing *is not* boring; then plan the day so that's the case.

RULE 4: Plan one major sight-seeing outing a day. Spend the rest of the time playing.

Time-outs are effective. The trick is to put the child in a totally boring environment for an allotted amount of time: the hotel room's bathroom; under a tree at a rest stop without any toys.

Jill Waterman practices avoidance whenever she can. She keeps games and toys on hand to distract her kids, hoping to keep fights at bay. "When you can," she adds, "it's helpful to not have them sit next to each other."

Individual tape players help too. (Kids can't trade insults if they can't hear them.) Of course, time apart is the best antidote. If tensions are really high in the car, stop for a few minutes and let youngsters take a break. Buy a candy bar or throw the ball for

---

RULE 5: Don't head out without eating and without a backpack with some healthy snacks and drinks. Hunger will strike at the oddest moments.

RULE 6: Always take a stroller for a child under four (or a backpack for a baby or toddler).

RULE 7: If the kids are different ages and have special interests, agree on the ground rules beforehand. If possible, divide up the family and head in different directions to accommodate everyone's desires.

RULE 8: No matter how much the kids complain, don't forgo what you want to do and see—not entirely anyway. Frequently, your enthusiasm and interest will spill over onto the kids.

RULE 9: No matter how much you've planned and organized, be flexible enough to shift gears.

RULE 10: Relax and have fun. That's what you're there for. And that's what the kids will remember.

a while. In a plane, see whether it's possible for one of them to switch seats.

If you've arrived at your destination, split them up for an hour or two: Take one to the pool while the other goes somewhere else with Dad or Grandma. Just being apart for a while—and given the opportunity to vent their frustrations—may be all that's needed to diffuse the situation.

You should be careful not to take sides in sibling squabbles. Listen to the problem, give them a ground rule for solving it, and then let them resolve the conflict on their own. For example, suggests Waterman, if they're arguing over which movie to watch in the hotel room, "Tell them the TV is off until they can come up with a plan."

If they're fighting about who sits where in the car, let them suggest a rotating system of assigned seats. "I remember when we were kids, we always drew imaginary lines on the seats to guard our territory," one young mother recalls.

You may laugh, but allowing the kids to have their own territory—no matter how small—frequently helps.

Reluctant travelers are another problem for vacationing families. On one of our vacations, Matt, our ten-year-old, couldn't have cared less about seeing San Francisco's sites. "Can't I just stay here at the hotel and watch TV all day?" he begged. "I'm glad I came today," Matt finally admitted over a bowl of clam chowder for lunch.

At one point or another, every family finds itself grappling with a reluctant traveler. It's aggravating, frustrating, and enough to make you think about putting away the suitcases and maps forever.

Don't. "Remember that kids who learn how to travel well are learning how to move about the world successfully," explains Dr. Bennett Leventhal, a child psychiatrist and chief of the University of Chicago Department of Psychiatry.

They're gaining confidence and a broader perspective than they get from life in their own neighborhood. They learn the value of trying new things. They meet interesting people, even seeing different sides of their parents and siblings than they do at home. They try new foods.

That's not to say kids won't need a little nudge in the right direction. For example, teenagers, who particularly like to feel they've got some freedom and control over their lives, are quick to dismiss any idea a parent has suggested. "Teenagers will tell you they're bored even if they're not," Dr. Leventhal laughs. Give them plenty of latitude. Perhaps they'd prefer a burger in the room instead of eating out with you. Perhaps they want to skip that art museum in favor of an afternoon at the beach. Perhaps they want to get together with other teens they've met snow-boarding, instead of skiing with you.

Families who have teens suggest it's smart to vacation where there will be a group of other teenagers around. "We had to remind her to spend time with the family," said Californian Michelle Spiegel.

On the other hand, teens might surprise you by the amount of time they will spend with you away from home, when there's not nearly as much competition for their time and attention. "We're always going in so many different directions at home," notes one Minnesota mother of two teenaged boys. "On vacation, we really get some time together as a family."

Some children may be reluctant to travel because they are afraid. "Before hitting the road, give fearful kids lots of reassurance that you'll be with them," suggests Chicago child psychologist Sharon Berry.

See whether there's a reason for their fear, adds Dr. Leventhal. Are they worried about a plane crash? An earthquake? Getting lost? Tell them you'll keep them safe.

Trial runs can help fearful kids. For example, if you plan to visit some large tourist attractions or historic sites, spend an afternoon at a similar local attraction first so the kids get used to the crowds and lines.

If they're particularly fearful of some activity—a roller-coaster, water slide, a ski lift to the top of the mountain—don't force the issue. "If you force them, everyone will be miserable," warns Maureen Mepham, a suburban Chicago nursery school teacher who has had many years of experience coaxing children to try new things. "Wait until they're ready."

12

Earaches, Sniffles, and Worse

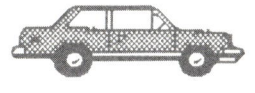

The Firemans had barely gotten to their San Diego hotel when the stomach flu struck with a vengeance. Ultimately, the beleaguered family packed up and headed back home to Los Angeles. "You can't drag sick kids around," says Jeffrey Fireman, a pediatrician. "They'll be miserable and so will you."

The Firemans were lucky that they could easily get home, though it ruined their plans for a relaxing weekend away. Too often, kids—and parents—get sick hundreds of miles from home, sometimes in foreign countries.

It's no wonder. Kids don't get enough sleep on vacation. They don't eat right. They may breathe stale airplane air for hours or sit next to someone with a bad cold. "No matter where you go on vacation, people are going to get sick. And kids are much more susceptible," Dr. Fireman says.

Airplanes aren't the only things that cause illness, of course. A sudden change of climate or a frenetic schedule can be responsible. A child can fall and break an arm or need stitches.

No matter how minor the illness or injury, it can be unnerving, disruptive, and even frightening when the family is far from home.

You might not be able to fly home if a child gets an ear infection, for fear the changing air pressure could harm his eardrum. You might have to cancel plans to leave the baby with a sitter if she's developed a fever.

Wherever you are when a child gets sick, try to reach your own pediatrician at home first, doctors urge, because he or she could coordinate the treatment or may know a colleague in the area you're visiting.

Ask friends or relatives for a local referral if your child needs to be seen there. Hotel officials also have families and could refer you to their doctors. You can always go to a local children's hospital emergency room.

If you're overseas, call the American embassy or local consulate. Travel medicine specialists suggest you ask there for a referral and a hospital where English is spoken. Even better, go armed with the names of English-speaking doctors and a major medical institution.

Carry all prescriptions for medications with you. This should include acetaminophen, a thermometer, bandages, adhesive tape, Band-Aids, antibiotic cream, antiseptic soap, tweezers, small scissors, and syrup of ipecac (for use in cases of poisoning but only after consultation with a physician).

Many families never leave home without over-the-counter remedies for colds, motion sickness, and diarrhea for parents and kids (check with your doctor first before giving to the kids), insect repellent and lotion to stop itching, sunscreen and lip balm, cotton swabs and balls, and alcohol in a plastic bottle.

If a child has a chronic condition like asthma, bad allergies, or diabetes, bring the medications you might need and medical records. Get the name and phone number of a specialist in the city you'll be visiting.

Pediatricians suggest parents think hard before taking young children to tiny Caribbean islands or other exotic spots. Babies can quickly develop a high fever or get dehydrated, and they may not be fully immunized against exposure to diseases in developing countries. Discuss your plans with your doctor before going. You also might want to carry a bottle of Pedialyte or another oral rehydration solution in your suitcase. "People need to have a plan in case their child gets sick," urges one doctor. "And they've got to be aware of the risks."

---

5 *Overseas Smarts*

If you plan to travel overseas, you should know that the Centers for Disease Control has established an International Travelers Hotline that provides information twenty-four hours a day. Call 404-639-8106. You can also call the International Association for Medical Assistance to Travelers, a worldwide organization of hospitals where English is spoken. Call 716-754-4883.

To keep everyone healthy when visiting developing countries like Mexico:

- Drink only bottled water or hot beverages
- Eat only fruits you have peeled yourself
- Don't sample street vendors' wares or eat raw vegetables
- Be sure foods are well cooked and arrive hot
- Avoid raw shellfish, fish, or undercooked meat

The faster you start treatment, the better. That's why when you think a child is coming down with something, you shouldn't wait until just before you leave for the airport to call the doctor. If you've reached your destination, don't wait until the situation has developed into a teeth-gnashing middle-of-the-night emergency before seeking medical help.

"It's a lot less expensive to go to the doctor," observes Fireman, "than having to change all of your family's vacation plans."

On one New Mexico ski trip, my son started complaining of an earache the first afternoon we were on the mountain. Once he got started on antibiotics—and spent a day playing games by the fire—he was fine.

13

Surviving the Holiday Crush

Rev up that holiday spirit. So what if the highway is slick with new snow? So what if your flight already has been delayed four hours? So what if the kids are griping, your spouse is whining, and you've got a cold?

Of course you hate holiday travel. Who wouldn't? But you can't stay home. Your in-laws are expecting you. The ski condo was paid for three months ago. And you traded favors for a month to get the time off work. So get with the program! There are a few easy ways to make holiday travel less difficult.

When traveling at holiday times, try to hit the road—or the airport—either before or after the peak travel days. It will be considerably less crowded—and less stressful.

Be prepared to wait—and wait some more. Give the kids one present they really want before you leave home so they have something to play with along the way. Make it a family tradition to bring a new game everyone can enjoy together when you arrive at your destination. If you're going to Grandma's, bring a holiday book for Grandma or Grandpa to read. Stash a few stocking stuffers in the bottom of the bag. Sing along with some holiday tapes in the car. This will brighten everyone's spirits. Use those long hours at the airport to read the kids a classic Christmas story. You might actually finish Dickens's *A Christmas Carol* this year!

Dredge up every hokey story you can remember from the holidays when you were a kid. The dumber they are, the more the kids will like them. How about the time you finally figured out the truth about Santa Claus?

If you still have Santa believers in your midst, tell them an elaborate tale of how Santa will find you—wherever you'll be. Produce a letter from Santa telling you to have a good trip, that he'll see you at Uncle Joe's house.

Take the time in the car or plane to go over "Present Etiquette" once again (i.e., no matter how much they hate what they get, just say thank you). Remind everyone to be diplomatic about their reactions about what's served at mealtimes. If the kids are picky eaters, a phone call ahead to discuss food might help forestall some embarrassing moments. Got a jar of peanut butter in the suitcase?

Whether you're going from warm weather to cold or the other way around, dress the kids and yourselves in comfortable layers that you can pull off or add on.

More than any other time of year, illness can strike suddenly. Keep tissues, acetaminophen, and any medicines your child might need for a chronic condition like asthma at close hand.

When you get to your destination, remember that despite parents' and grandparents' best efforts, a holiday dinner is not going to be an elegant gourmet feast—not with a gaggle of kids around anyway. Mix the stress of travel with the strain of family relationships and you can't expect the gathering around the holiday table to be the Norman Rockwell picture you had in mind.

Still, when it comes to the holidays, we all jump through expensive and exhausting hoops to be together around the table, spilling red wine on snowy white tablecloths and eating cholesterol-laden foods we wouldn't touch at home.

"There are fewer and fewer opportunities to be together," explains Syracuse University psychologist Barbara Fiese, an expert in family rituals who travels cross-country to be with her family. "At least one time a year we can focus on being together."

The first rule for a successful holiday family dinner is don't make the kids wait all day for a meal. Have food on hand during the day—cheese and crackers, veggies and dip. And when it's finally time to sit down, make sure there are some things on the menu that kids will eat: plain turkey, mashed potatoes, simple vegetables, and desserts like ice cream and cookies. A phone call ahead to the host or hostess might help ease any tensions over plates that go back to the kitchen still piled with food.

It also helps to dress the kids in casual clothes. You won't be nervous they'll ruin that "special" outfit, and the kids will be far more comfortable—especially without their parents watching their every move.

No matter what their ages, give children plenty of space away from the dinner table. "They want to eat and then they want to play," explains Chicago child psychologist Sharon Berry. "They don't want to spend an hour and a half sitting at the table," especially these days when families typically don't spend more than fifteen or twenty minutes eating a meal together. When the kids are done, excuse them from the table. Call them back when it's time for dessert. The Stiers family gathers every Thanksgiving on one relative's Missouri farm. The kids eat earlier than the adults—and then go out and jump in the hay. The adults can enjoy their dinner while the kids play outside.

It's better to plan an activity everyone can enjoy together before dinner than count on the dining table to provide the togetherness you're seeking.

Don't assume, however, that the kids will get along famously, especially if they don't know one another well or haven't seen one another for a long time.

Plan something to help them get through that awkward time right after they first arrive. Have a willing uncle teach them a new card game or some magic tricks. Suggest they prepare a talent show for after-dinner entertainment.

Assigned jobs can help too—and make it easier on those getting the meal ready. Have one group make cranberry sauce while another sets the table and a third draws place cards. Older kids are usually willing to look after the younger ones—especially if you offer to pay them for the service.

"The idea is to get everyone relaxed and involved," explains Susan Ginsberg, a New York educational consultant. "Do whatever you can to make it all easier."

That's my favorite Thanksgiving recipe.

III

Family Matters

14

Work and Play

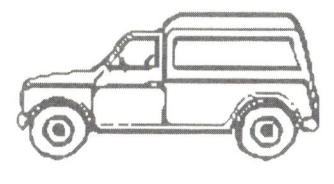

Kids toting briefcases?

All across the country, busy working parents are trying to sandwich in a little extra family time by taking the kids along on business trips—so many that 43 million business trips now include a child, the U.S. Travel Data Center reports. "People seem much more accepting of children being around," says Terry Henson, managing director of two Orlando, Florida, Holiday Inns that offer free licensed day care.

Some parents take the kids when the trip is more junket than work, like a seminar at a resort. Other times, the opportunity to introduce a child to a foreign city may be too good to resist. Occasionally, parents have no choice.

Bob and Lisa McClure must frequently attend the same meetings, so they bring their young daughter Missy along. If they don't have a sitter on hand, McClure says, "My wife would go to the reception for a while and then I'd go." Other times, friends pinch-hit.

"I think having the kids along sets a tone," observes parent Al Capizzi. "They see I'm a guy who really cares about my family."

Financial writer Brad Schade agrees. "Having Megan along at the convention was a great ice-breaker," he said. "People would come up to us and tell stories about their own kids."

Child development experts say such trips are good for the kids too. They get to see their parents in a different role than at home and benefit by the chance to glimpse the adult work world. "They get to see what I do and I get them involved helping," Al Capizzi says. "They see what work is. Their teachers thought it was great." Matt Kolsky, a suburban Chicago teenager who watched his father lead a workshop on the East Coast, says, "I didn't figure a business meeting could be interesting. But when you catch on to what they're saying, it's really interesting."

Of course, parents should choose their opportunities wisely. Tense negotiating sessions probably wouldn't be a good time to bring kids. Parents should also make sure colleagues—and bosses—have no objections to the arrangement.

Make sure the kids are prepared too. They need to understand that Mom or Dad must get their work done before they can have fun together. Are the kids willing and old enough to stay alone in a hotel room for a few hours? If not, make sure you

---

1 📁 *At a Convention*

Two companies that now offer children's activities at meetings are San Diego–based KiddieCorp (819-455-1718) and New Orleans–based Accents on Arrangements (504-524-1227).

Both companies provide activities for children during business meetings at hotels around the country.

have a sitter you can count on. Joannie Flynn, for example, brought her husband on one trip to Hawaii so that he could watch the kids; at other times, she enrolls the kids in hotel children's activities while she attends her meetings. "The kids always have a great time when they go with me," she says.

Meeting planners report increased demand for children's programs. Companies have sprung up specifically to provide such services. If you're heading to a convention, don't wait until you get there to determine what children's activities will be available. If many people are bringing their kids, ask the meeting planner to arrange activities and child care.

If activities are available, make sure to ask whether your kids are old enough to participate. Ask what kind of activities are planned, the cost, and the hours they will be offered. Ask whether extra baby-sitting is available if needed. "If they offer children's programs, it increases attendance at meetings," observes Hilton executive Joannie Flynn, who frequently has taken her two kids with her on business trips.

"It's a way to pay back the family for some of the inconveniences business travel can cause," adds Flynn, who lives in Los Angeles. "And it helps keep my life in balance on the road."

Taking the kids has a downside, of course. While some parents say they don't worry as much about their children if they're with them, there won't be any respite from responsibilities when you get back to your hotel room. Younger kids might balk at going to organized activities or staying with a strange sitter. Even worse, you'll be more tempted than ever to play hookey.

15

Just the Two of Us

The ambiance was perfect in the tiny dining room, from the snowy white tablecloths to the candlelight to the bud vase in the center of the table. We smiled at each other across the seafood fettuccine and steamed clams—that "how did I get so lucky with you" kind of secret smile.

Then my daughter Reggie, in between bites, filled me in on the latest doings in her second-grade class.

We were in Bisbee, Arizona, just the two of us, in the midst of a research trip for one of my books. With her teacher's blessing and a packet of homework in her backpack, Reggie had joined me for the ten-day trip. We spent more time alone together than we had since she was born.

We rode horses amid the cactus in Tucson, browsed the galleries in Santa Fe, explored the underground mine in Bisbee, and gawked at the sparkling formations deep in Carlsbad Caverns. We toured museums, shared greasy burgers, and cuddled up at night in a double bed while I read Nancy Drew mysteries aloud.

For a middle child in a family with two working parents who complains she never gets enough "alone" time with either Mom or Dad, the trip proved the perfect antidote. Reggie had plenty of time in the car to list every grievance against her older brother and younger sister. She told me the latest gossip from school. I told her stories about when I was a kid. We tried to outdo each other telling corny jokes.

I reveled in our time together as much as she did. Reggie was funny, cooperative, and patient as I interviewed people along the way. Map in hand, she helped navigate. She rarely whined, not even when I got us hopelessly lost. She was hardly ever grumpy, despite long hours in the car. She did her schoolwork dutifully, even keeping a journal of each day's events. Where was this child at home? I wondered.

"The dynamics are all different," one psychologist explained to me later. "You're focused on each other rather than on chores and work and homework. You're more like companions, not parent and child."

Patt Murray agrees. Owner of a Chicago area hair salon, she's frequently traveled alone with her teenaged son since he was small. "It's like he's taking care of me too," she explains. "There's a special bond when you discover new things together."

Not every moment will be wonderful, however. Like any couple traveling together, you'll have your spats. But you may find that you'll resolve them quickly, with a lot less pouting than at home.

Of course, you won't have anyone to help shoulder your adult burdens when things go wrong. "You're always on duty. You can never totally relax," notes Patt Murray. But in retrospect, that may seem a small price to pay for the time together.

Away from the pressures of life at home, your world is both smaller—and bigger. The change from daily routine is what makes trips alone with a child so special—and memorable. "It was like sitting back and looking at the big picture," recalls

Washington, D.C., administrator Cathi Hanna, who took her kindergartner with her on a business trip. "We talked a lot. He was very funny—and grown-up."

Child development experts explain that a parent's time alone with one child can have long-lasting benefits for the entire family. Children need to feel they are appreciated for themselves, as individuals. They need to feel heard, that their parents are really listening to them. Vacations are the perfect opportunity to help a child develop this confidence. Even an afternoon foray together at home or in the midst of a vacation can work wonders.

"It was so nice to focus on one child at a time. You can be attuned to them as a person, not just one of the kids," says one mother who took a short trip with her eldest.

"Times like that are so special to a child," agrees pediatrician Diane Holmes, recalling the annual Christmas shopping excursion she, the only girl in the family, shared with her father.

2 　 Time Away Together

Time away together doesn't have to be anything exotic or expensive. All that matters is the chance to spend some easygoing time together. It's worth the effort. You can do it on vacation with the entire family or even at home:

- Go out for breakfast with one child while the rest of the family sleeps in
- Have the oldest child caddie when you're playing golf
- Hit the shopping mall with your daughter while Dad and the other kids go to the playground
- Go for a walk together after dinner
- Play games just for two, like cards, checkers, or chess

The intrinsic message is that Mom or Dad wants to be with them, just them alone; that they're not just along for the ride. Siblings will feel less compelled to compete for parents' attention. Adolescents will grow up knowing they can talk to their parents.

"But remember to plan with the child in mind," cautions Carey Halsey, who teaches child development at Loyola-Stritch University Medical School in Chicago. "Let the children take the lead."

You may have such a good time that your child won't want to go home. Reggie cried all the way home on the airplane. I resolved to make more "alone" time for her every week. But I'm not sure that's enough for her. I think she'd like the two of us to take off again—permanently.

16

That First Trip as a Single Parent

Suzy Marta was terrified. She thought people were staring at her and her sons because they didn't have a father with them. She was sure they'd get a flat tire. She was convinced the boys would have a terrible time. That first brief trip with her kids after her divorce turned out to be far more fun than Suzy ever expected and far more significant. "It was very important for us to take a step like that and see that we were still a family," she explains. "Though that trip was just a weekend, it showed the boys—and me—that I could do things on my own. It was healing for all of us."

Suzy and her sons went on to take some memorable trips—camping in the West, white-water river rafting, and visits to Disney World. They were always on a tight budget but always managed to have a good time.

She laughs about the anxiety that first trip provoked. But those feelings of insecurity are all too common among single parents, experts say.

"Go even if you do it on the cheap," advises Suzy. "It's OK if you don't have all the answers. Just keep your sense of humor."

These days, single parents will have plenty of company wherever they go. There are more than 10 million single-parent families—almost a third of all families in the nation with children.

One way to make traveling as a single parent easier is to go someplace like a resort or ranch where there will be organized activities and plenty of kids around. For families who can afford it, Club Med is a popular choice. So are cruises. Some ships and resorts now offer special pricing for single parents.

"You want a situation where you can get a break too," explains Susan Kennedy, a therapist who treats many divorced families.

But don't go expecting to find romance. "I always had to go back to the room at night with my son," laughs one single attorney. On the other hand, if you're meeting new people on vacation, the kids can help break the ice. "You can relax and

---

3 Support Services

Several organizations around the country offer support and information on a variety of subjects for families grappling with divorce, single parenting, and stepfamily issues. Call:

- Rainbows, for programs for children of divorce and those who have lost parents or siblings (708-310-1880)
- The Stepfamilies Association of America (800-735-0329)
- SingleMother, a newsletter for mothers raising children alone (704-888-KIDS)
- Parents Without Partners (800-637-7974)
- Mothers Without Custody; send a self-addressed stamped envelope to Box 27418, Houston, TX 77227

have a totally relaxed conversation with other adults without it being loaded in any way," says a New York mom.

Many single parents say visiting friends is an affordable option. "It's a great way to keep up with old friends and that's important when you're single," one Los Angeles mom explains.

Wherever you go, expect the kids to miss the parent who isn't there. They may even feel guilty for having a good time. Encourage them to write and call. Acknowledge their fears and discomfort about the situation. And don't feel compelled to keep busy every minute.

17

It's Not the Brady Bunch

No one could agree on what to do or when to do it. One stepdaughter cried the entire time. The rest of the crew was obviously not happy either: Their parents, exhausted and overwhelmed, didn't get the vacation they'd expected.

"We were totally ignoring what the children wanted and needed," ruefully says Jan Scharman, recalling that first trip after her remarriage, trying to blend two families into one. "We were so focused on trying to be one big happy family that we made a lot of mistakes."

That was several years ago. On their vacations since, Jan and Brent Scharman—who are both psychologists, have served on the board of the Stepfamilies Association of America, and have ten children between them—have tried to make the experience one the kids want to repeat, not avoid.

The couple has learned to involve the kids in the planning rather than just announce where they will all have to go, and to let them decide who will room with whom.

Just as important, they've learned that once on vacation, nobody in the family should be forced to do the same activity at the same time, from breakfast through dinner. "We've got very different kids," she explains. "They have different interests."

The more flexibility that can be built into a trip, the better. Stepparents around the country suggest seeking out vacation spots that will offer plenty of options—so the kids can go in different directions. Make sure there's some one-on-one time for each child with his or her biological parent too.

Blended families should take comfort in the knowledge that all of their efforts on vacation will be worth the trouble—and aggravation.

With families spread across the country and some stepchildren living hundreds of miles away, "vacations are a good way to get to know each other in a more relaxed environment," says Dr. Alberto Serrano, director of the Philadelphia Child Guidance Center and a professor of psychiatry at the University of Pennsylvania.

Other experts in the field stress that vacations provide a wonderful opportunity to share experiences and establish new traditions and rituals. Go to new places rather than to places where you vacationed as separate families. Try new activities so that everyone isn't just sitting around feeling uneasy and uncomfortable.

Realize, especially when a couple is newly married, that the kids may feel jealous of the new spouse. They might feel disloyal to their absent parent if they have a good time. They may feel they're missing something. Encourage them to call or send postcards.

"Don't compete with their other family," cautions Jan Scharman. "Openly talk about the fun they have with them."

Be aware that the stepfamily may have a different style of vacationing. Your stepkids might sleep late while your kids are used to being up with the sun; they might want to eat in when your kids are used to eating out. It's a good idea to talk about those issues with all of the kids before the trip.

"The children are going to feel strange at first," says Dr. Serrano. "They're not normally together and if there's a big age difference, they have no reason to want to be together. It all puts a lot of pressure on parents. The challenge is to plan carefully."

And keep your expectations low. Despite your hopes, it won't feel like "The Brady Bunch on Vacation," not the first couple of trips anyway. "I don't know any stepfamily relationship that's perfect," observes JoAnn Fox-Avnet, a Los Angeles psychologist who treats many such families and is part of a stepfamily herself.

Newer blended families might want to opt for a long weekend at first instead of a longer trip. Don't be concerned if the kids are moody or withdrawn at the start. By the time they go home, they should be smiling. Explains Jan Scharman: "If they leave with a good feeling, they'll want to come back."

18

When the Kids Don't Live with You

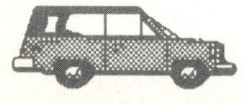

Jennifer Isham has one rule when her sons arrive to visit. "I don't kiss them at the airport. That embarrasses them."

Her kids visit just twice a year from across the country, and no matter how much she's missed them, she plays it low-key at first, giving them plenty of time to watch TV and even come with her to the market to be sure she buys all of their favorite brands.

"Look for the little joys," she suggests. "Try not to hang all of your hopes and expectations on one visit."

That can be especially difficult over the holidays, an often trying time for divorced families.

Remember that no family vacation—even in the happiest two-parent family—is perfect. When parents and children haven't seen each other or spent much concentrated time together in months, it's even more difficult. Parents must adjust to how the kids may have changed. The kids will fight and push the limits of behavior.

Every year at Christmastime and over the summer the same scenes are being played out across the country as millions of children visit and vacation with the parent they don't normally live with. These families are becoming an increasingly visible presence everywhere, on cruise ships and beach resorts as well as on the ski slopes and in major tourist capitals.

"Too many single fathers get themselves in a rut with their kids," observes one Midwestern physician. "Travel adds a whole new dimension to your relationship. You're exploring new territory. It's not only exciting, it's some of the best times I have had."

He notes that people give them the royal treatment wherever they go. "They think it's great to see a father traveling along with his children."

"Don't not go because you're afraid it will be too hard," says a divorced father of four from Los Angeles who has traveled cross-country with his brood. "The kids' excitement about spending all of the time with you will make it all go well."

Don't feel it's necessary to treat the kids to an expensive vacation either. Dr. Barry Nurcombe, a Vanderbilt University child psychiatrist and spokesperson for the American Academy of Child and Adolescent Psychiatry, says, "The best time is spent doing something parent and child both like, when the child has your undivided attention."

Go fishing, build something, paint a room, he suggests. "Use the time to talk about how life is going."

Even though the kids don't live with you, you can still involve them in planning the vacation. Call and ask them what they'd like to do. They may not want to go skiing. They might have a big party the weekend you want to take them camping. They shouldn't feel they're simply being told what to do or where to go.

Before you head off someplace, spend a few days with them at home. This will give you all time to adjust to one another's company. Don't let them feel like guests in your home. Ask them to do the dishes, make their beds—all the things they would do if they lived there full time. You want kids to feel a sense of family, the experts explain. That means giving them a space where they can stash their clothes and toothbrush and keep to a structured routine.

Try not to be critical of your ex-spouse either. That won't help anyone. "Let the old animosities live where they should, in the past," offers Professor Lewis Lopsitt, founder of Brown University's Child Studies Center.

19

Joining Forces

It could be the perfect vacation: The kids have live-in playmates. Parents share child care and housekeeping chores, keeping costs down in the process.

No wonder growing numbers of families are choosing to join forces with another family on vacation. They're renting houses on Cape Cod and cabins in the Colorado mountains, ski condos in Utah, beach condos in Florida. They're pitching tents side-by-side in national parks.

Some go away with neighbors or parents of their children's friends. Others take the opportunity to see old college or childhood buddies who now live hundreds or thousands of miles away.

"You get to catch up on each other's lives," says Anne Reams, who heads to the Florida beach with three couples—all boyhood friends of her husband's—and all of their kids. "You gab. You cook together. You clean up together. But it's not a vacation where you spend a lot of time with your own family."

"It's great for a single parent," says Chicago attorney Lynn Heistand, who shares a beach house every year with a friend and has headed to resorts with other families. "The kids have each other and I have companionship too."

"The kids are off playing together and it's as if we're out by ourselves," says Californian Laura Sutherland. No need to entertain a couple of squabbling siblings all evening.

With more adults around, parents can divvy up the kids during the day so everyone has more options of things to do. One dad can take them sailing while a mom heads to the beach; another dad might lead a group fishing while his wife takes the others on a hike.

Of course, such arrangements do have drawbacks. Are you sure there's enough space to go around so that you feel comfortable? Some families pile all of the kids in one room. That's easiest on the budget but not always on the nerves. Who gets the best bedroom? Others opt for separate units to avoid such issues.

However you divide the space, make sure to talk about the arrangements—and how you'll spend your days and evenings—before sending in the deposit.

"This kind of trip could ruin a friendship," laughs Reams. "Make sure you really know the people you're traveling with."

Different styles are fine—as long as each family can accommodate the other and discuss differences before heading out. How will you feel if one of the other parents yells at your son or gives orders to your daughter? Philadelphia child psychologist Marion Lindblad-Goldberg suggests it helps if the kids have a relationship beforehand or are at least close in age. If the families aren't close friends or don't see each other often, it's always wise to opt for a place that offers plenty of activities where everyone can get away from one another.

How will you handle finances? Some groups keep a running tab and divvy up expenses at the end; others throw money into a kitty and add more when it gets low. Find a simple system everyone is comfortable with.

"You don't want to worry about who's eating all of the Oreos or drinking more beer," says Anne Reams. You also don't want to get your nose out of joint because you feel like you're pulling all the kitchen duty. "Decide ahead who will be responsible for which dinners," suggests Laura Sutherland.

4 Roomy Accommodations

Forget being crowded in too-small hotel rooms that cost too much. Condo-renting is economical and roomy. Even parents get a modicum of privacy. And there's no need to face restaurants three times a day with the kids. No wonder so many families insist that renting condos or houses is the only way to travel.

Adventurous families swap houses with counterparts in other regions or other countries, paying a modest fee to have their house listed but largely negating the cost of lodging away from home. Sometimes they even trade cars and housekeepers. An added plus: the chance to live temporarily in a neighborhood as opposed to a tourist area. The kids might even make some friends on the block!

Many agencies now specialize in these kind of arrangements. For condo or villa rental in the United States, Caribbean, Mexico, and abroad, try:

- HIDEAWAYS (800-843-4433)
- Condominium Travel Associates (213-975-7714)
- Interhome (201-882-6864)

For house-swapping call:

- The Vacation Exchange Club (800-638-3841)
- Intervac U.S./International Home Exchanger (800-756-HOME)

Don't forget to plan some excursions alone with your family, even just for a couple of hours. You'll all need the break—and a good sense of humor.

Another fun way to join forces is to travel with members of your extended family. Such intergenerational vacations offer scattered families a chance to be together in a relaxed setting, feeling again that all-powerful sense of belonging.

Vacations like those are gaining popularity as '90s families seek ways to stay close, despite thousands of miles and different lifestyles. Upscale and budget resorts, cruise lines, and hotels offer "reunion packages" to make the planning all the easier—on the wallet too.

Many families now stage mammoth reunions every few years at various locales, drawing hundreds together to celebrate their heritage. "Definitely do it before it's too late," advises Lynaie Bergman from North Dakota, whose family—all 162 of them—gathered in Colorado. "We feel like we're passing on the family history this way."

"One of the real attractions is that the cousins get to know each other," says Hollywood screenwriter Jeff Melvoin, whose siblings and parents have gathered to ski, ride horses, and celebrate holidays together.

Trips with the entire family aren't easy to plan. It's difficult to organize around everyone's frenetic schedules and different budgets. It's smart to plan early. Designate one person to be the chief organizer and decision maker. Poll everyone to see where they'd like to go, when—and how much they've got to spend.

The farther out you plan, the better deal you can get—and wider choice of accommodations. For the best deals, travel off-season or in shoulder seasons, if you can.

Consider how long the family really wants to be together. Look for a place that offers activities that will appeal to a wide range of age groups. The kids have the beach while you've got first-rate tennis courts and your parents can golf every morning.

Don't make the mistake of thinking everyone must spend every moment together. And don't think everyone will get along better just because the scenery is spectacular and the food's good. The same thing that bugs you about your sister-in-law in Milwaukee will bother you on a cruise ship in the middle of the ocean or on top of a ski slope in Colorado.

5 *Reunion Countdown*

The YMCA of the Rockies' sprawling 840-acre Estes Park Center and Snow Mountain Ranch near Rocky Mountain National Park in Colorado host more than six hundred family reunions every year. There's even a staffer assigned to arrange activities for the families. Call 800-777-YMCA for details as well as tips on planning your reunion.

Here are some YMCA-suggested activities guaranteed to keep everyone happy—for a while anyway:

- Tell old family stories. Create a family history book with the old stories and anecdotes.

- Make bubbles in a big vat for the kids out of water and dishwashing detergent. Figure a gallon of water to one-third cup of detergent. (Joy and Dawn are said to work the best.) Make hangers into circles and squares. Dip your hands in the vat, spread your fingers, and blow!

- Stage a family Olympics with all kinds of goofy games. Can you shape your body into different letters of the alphabet? Have you ever tried passing a football with your feet?

- Solicit contributions to a family cookbook.

- Make a family tree and send everyone home with a copy.

- Get caps and T-shirts with the family name, date, and location of the reunion.

"Many of us haven't vacationed with our families since high school and now it's twenty years later," says one Northwestern University family therapist. "Remember it's going to be really different."

Everyone has got to bend and compromise to make such trips with other families successful.

20

Grandma, Get Ready!

Listen up, grandparents: This one's for you. Quick, put away those cherished collectibles and all the bottles of pills. Stock up on pizza, peanut butter, and chocolate chip cookies. Make sure the VCR works and get out those old favorite read-aloud books. Then sit back and get ready for chaos.

You'll get plenty of it as soon as the grandkids arrive for their visit. Of course, you're going to enjoy every hectic moment—most of them anyway.

Bite your tongue when you get angry at your grandkids' messes. Send them out to play when their noise gets overwhelming. Remember that today, when families live so far apart, these visits are more important than ever. Visiting Grandma and Grandpa helps kids understand their history and feel connected and loved. It's key to their self-esteem as kids and later as adults, experts explain.

"So just play with the kids and don't worry about getting any chores done," advises Ellen Cusack, a suburban Chicago

94 • *Family Matters*

grandma who has survived many such visits. "Tranquilizers wouldn't hurt," she jokes.

"You can't holler at kids you don't see that often," adds Ruth Lerner, who gets annual visits from her East Coast grandchildren at her southern California condo. Her advice: Forget picking up after them constantly.

Don't be miffed if the grandkids don't greet you with open arms. They might take some time to warm up—especially if they

---

6 *Safety Check*

Before that toddling visitor arrives, the National Safe Kids Campaign says grandparents should be sure of the following:

- A car seat is available for the car.
- The water heaters are set no higher than 120 degrees Fahrenheit.
- All guns are locked away.
- Emergency numbers, including the local poison control center, are placed near the phone.
- Vitamins, household cleaners, medicines, and matches are locked away.
- Pot handles are turned toward the back of the stove when cooking.
- Chairs and furniture are moved away from windows to discourage young climbers. Install window guards (available at most hardware stores) to prevent falls.
- Safety gates are installed at the top and bottom of stairs.
- Smoke detectors are working, and older kids know how to get out in case of fire.
- Small items that could cause choking—coins, batteries, small toys, jewelry—are stored out of reach.

haven't seen you in a while. Grandma and Grandpa will need time to adjust too.

"You get exhausted from all the noise," acknowledges Ruth Lerner. But it's easy to take a breather when they're outside playing. "That's when I sit down and relax," she says.

"You forget what it's like to have young kids around," agrees Ellen Cusack. "You can't turn your back on them for a minute."

If you're expecting crawlers, toddlers, or preschoolers, do a thorough safety check before they arrive. Are the household poisons and medicines out of reach (including those pills you keep in your purse)? Are the electric outlets plugged with safety covers? Have you picked up electrical cords from the floor? You don't want the baby chewing on them. At the holidays, be especially careful about Christmas lights and low-hanging ornaments. Try putting a barrier around the tree.

Invest in some inexpensive plastic plates and cups for the younger kids. That way you won't have to worry about your good china and glassware every time a child asks for juice.

Check ahead to see what foods and toys are favorites of the month and have a supply on hand. Plan some "special" activities. A ball game with Grandpa? Tea at a fancy hotel with Grandma? A big pancake breakfast? Invite older ones to visit without Mom and Dad. Plan a project you and the kids would enjoy doing together: working on the car, baking cookies, planting vegetables, rewiring a lamp.

But, cautions Chicago grandma Jerry Rosenthal, check ahead to make sure the kids—and their parents—approve the choices. Nothing is worse than investing in an expensive set of tickets to a basketball game or a ballet only to learn the kids have no interest in going.

Don't figure they'll want to go from cousin to aunt to old friend for visits either. Whatever their ages, they'll want lots of time simply to play. Jerry Rosenthal solves the "but everyone wants to see the kids" dilemma by hosting one get-together during the visit. Here's a good tip: Fix a place in the house where the kids can spread out and call their own. Put a TV there so they can watch early morning cartoons without disturbing anyone. Have a cache of markers, paper, books, and games on hand. A couple of balls are good bets for all ages. So are legos and puzzles. Buy a storybook for younger children and chapter book for older ones. Make time during the visit to read the "special" book together.

When the kids arrive, try to avoid being critical or judgmental about the way they dress, eat, or are being raised, urges Dr. Arthur Kornhaber, who started the Foundation for Grandparents, a nonprofit organization that's devoted to enhancing grandchild-grandparent relationships.

"Focus on the good things," he advises. Adapt to the kids' schedules and routines rather than expecting them to bend to yours. Leave the disciplining to the parents.

Use the time together to get to know the kids. Sit down and play cards with them or watch a favorite video together. Get out the old family albums. The kids will love seeing the pictures and hearing stories about when you—and their parents—were kids.

As grandchildren get older, more grandparents are opting to vacation with them without their parents. Grandparents and grandkids are cruising and relaxing at resorts and touring national parks. Grandtravel, a Maryland travel agency, specializes in such trips (call 800-247-7651).

Before heading out with the grandkids, talk about likes and dislikes. Do you sleep with the light on or off? Do you like big breakfasts or just a quick bite? Are museums or beaches your idea of a perfect place to spend the day?

And no matter how much you love the kids, pick a trip or destination where there will be other children—and grandparents—around. Everyone will be happier.

21

Time for Romance

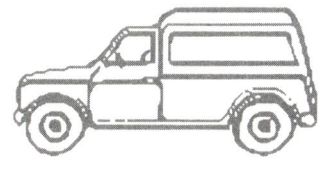

The kids were as ready for a break from us as we were from them after an afternoon touring the Kennedy Space Center in Florida coupled with several hours in the car.

That's why once we settled into the hotel, we ordered them a room service dinner—a real treat in their book—set them up for a pay TV movie, waited until four-year-old Melanie was asleep, and then headed downstairs for a blissfully relaxing late dinner by ourselves.

They were just as pleased with their evening as we were with ours. At eleven and nine, Matt and Reggie were thrilled we trusted them enough to stay with their younger sister for a couple of hours. We left them armed with the restaurant phone number right in the hotel, but they didn't call once. All were asleep when we returned.

As we headed down the elevator that night to our decidedly adult meal, I realized I didn't feel guilty for wanting to escape my brood, much as I love them, for a couple of hours. The next morning, my husband and I both felt energized, looking forward to the day ahead with the kids at Disney World. The kids were just as upbeat.

That's exactly what's supposed to happen, psychologists and marital counselors say. Breaks from the kids, even on vacation, are good for everyone. The children need to see that parents' lives involve more than just being Mom and Dad. Older kids

7 Kid-Friendly Hotels

Here are some hotels that are offering various children's programs at some of their properties:

- Club Med (800-CLUB MED)
- Embassy Suites (800-EMBASSY)
- Hilton (800-934-1000)
- Holiday Inn Sunspree Resorts (800-HOLIDAY)
- Hyatt Resorts (800-233-1234)
- Marriott (800-228-9290)
- Sheraton (800-325-3535)
- Sonesta (800-SONESTA)
- Westin (800-228-3000)

And a few individual family-friendly resorts around the country:

- The Alisal, Santa Barbara, California (800-4-ALISAL)
- The Boca Raton Resort and Beach Club in Florida (800-327-0101)
- Disney World Resorts (407-W-DISNEY)
- Kutsher's Country Club, New York (914-794-6000)
- MGM Grand Las Vegas (800-929-1111)

want a chance to prove they're responsible enough to be on their own, for a few hours anyway. Parents need the time to recharge their relationship and take a breather from the twenty-four-hour togetherness that's considerably more intense than everyone's comings and goings at home.

Traditionally vacations were supposed to spur romance, even for long-married couples. But any parent knows it's difficult to manage much "couple time" with the kids around.

- The Rancho Bernardo Inn, San Diego (800-542-6096)
- Smuggler's Notch, Vermont (800-451-8752)
- The Tyler Place Highgage Springs, Vermont (802-868-3301)

RASCALS IN PARADISE puts together family trips complete with a counselor along to arrange children's activities. Call 800-U-RASCAL.

In the Caribbean and Hawaii:

- Aston Hotels, Hawaii (800-922-7866)
- Bitter End Yacht Club, Virgin Gorda, British Virgin Islands (800-872-2392)
- Boscobal Beach, Jamaica (800-858-8009)
- Club Med (800-CLUB MED)
- The FDR Resort, Jamaica (800-654-1FDR)
- Grand Wailea Resort, Maui (800-888-6100)
- Palmas del Mar, Puerto Rico (800-468-3331)
- Ritz Carleton, Hawaii (800-845-9905)
- Sapphire Beach, St. Thomas (800-524-2090)
- Windjammer Landing, St. Lucia (800-243-1166)

"Parents need to put energy into it," says Northwestern University marital therapist Karen Abrams. "The need [for time together] is no different than at home."

It takes some planning, though, especially when the kids are small.

Some families recruit a young niece, cousin, or neighbor to join the group as a baby-sitter. They're usually thrilled to be invited along, all too glad to help care for the younger children in return for a trip to Disney World, the beach, or a ski resort.

Splurge on a second room for part of the trip. You can build it into your budget, and the extra space—not to mention the chance to steal a few minutes alone—is worth every penny. Some hotel chains, Hyatts among them, offer half-price rates for a second room for the kids.

Frequently, young employees at ski or beach resorts are only too glad to earn some extra money baby-sitting. Ask at the children's ski school or hotel activities' desk.

Make sure to find out how the hotel checks out these sitters, whether they are hotel employees and whether they have references and first-aid training. Ask the hotel concierge the name of his or her favorite sitter. Make sure you're clear on the fees ahead of time, since hotel sitters tend to be expensive.

Another solution is hotel-arranged children's activities. Whatever the family's budget or earmarked destination, there have never been so many programs for children—from toddlers to teens—offered at large resorts and hotels as well as small family-run places. They couldn't be more different than baby-sitting. The kids can wind-surf or fish, throw mud on a pottery wheel and make jewelry, learn Spanish, or even try their hand at cooking some regional favorites.

Hoteliers know today's kids want action from morning until night. "If it sounds and smells like baby-sitting, my three boys are the first to leave," says Las Vegas attorney Bob Unger, who travels frequently with his family.

A growing number of programs are designed for teens too—teen discos or rooms set aside where they can just gather to watch TV, video arcades or daylong adventures tailored for their age groups.

At the same time, as kids become more expert at various sports, resorts are responding with an ever-growing range of lessons that enable kids to work on their skills with teachers who volunteer and are specially trained to teach young skiers, sailors, or divers, among others.

It'll be easier for you to work in some R&R knowing that the kids are busy having fun. Hit the expert slopes while they get a snow-boarding lesson. Scuba dive while they snorkel. Snooze by the pool while your toddler finger-paints, or enjoy dinner while the kids watch a flick with a group their own age.

"The kids didn't even want to leave for dinner they were having so much fun," Unger says.

Of course, some parents hate the concept. "The idea is to go on vacation to be with your kids," one grouses.

But if this is the only vacation you'll get, you deserve some time off too. The key is to pick the program that's right for your family—and your budget. Some families book the kids into activities every minute of their vacation. Others opt for just a few hours, both to give themselves a break and to give different-aged kids a chance to do what they want.

It's important to ask a lot of questions before booking. Some of the programs are seasonal; others operate year-round. Some are complimentary, like the one at San Diego's Rancho Bernardo Inn, or included in the resort fee, while others cost upwards of fifty dollars a day per child. Some accept babies, like certain Club Meds, but others have no activities for children until they're out of diapers and in school. Some have evening activities.

Ask to see the schedule for the week to determine how many different activities will be offered. Inquire about staff qualifications and the ratio of counselors to children. If you're traveling at peak periods, find out whether it's necessary to reserve a spot for each child. What kinds of meals and snacks will be offered?

Off season, make sure the activities are ongoing. Call ahead and talk to someone directly involved in the program, not just a reservations agent.

There's one snag, though: The kids may not buy into the idea as readily as you do. My kids, for example, wouldn't consider heading off to a kids' program in Florida when they could spend the entire day with me, jumping the waves in the ocean.

Don't assume a three-year-old or a shy nine-year-old will gladly spend all day among strangers. Younger ones overwhelmed by a new environment might not be comfortable letting you out of their sight.

Even if you're committed to the idea and you've chosen the spot specifically because of the children's program, make sure the kids know you'll be flexible and won't force their participation.

If this seems like a lot of trouble to get a little couple time, remember it's worth the effort. How well parents get along can directly influence their children's happiness.

IV

Vacations Everyone Will Enjoy

22

Hitting the Slopes

"Follow us," the kids commanded. Then they took off down the mountain without looking back.

"I think this is the last year I can keep up with them," my husband said, breathless at the bottom.

I didn't even try, inadvertently giving my crew plenty of ammunition for their jokes about Mom's "pokey" pace. Rather than being insulted, though, I was pleased that they were skiing well enough to give their parents a run for their money—and having so much fun doing it.

At ages nine and eleven, Reggie and Matt were wonderfully at ease on their skis, confident they could handle any run. Not bad for a couple of Midwestern kids lucky to ski a week a season.

The secret to their success on the slopes? Letting them perfect their skills at their own pace, improving a bit each season. Of course, our enthusiasm for the sport helped. They wanted to learn to ski because we enjoyed it so much. Their younger sister, in turn, was thrilled when she was old enough to start because she wanted to keep pace with her older siblings.

Skiing is a wonderful, albeit expensive, sport for families to share and one they can enjoy together for a lifetime. That's all the more reason to give the kids plenty of time to learn.

"Forcing it won't work," says Steamboat Ski School director Rick Devos. "Too many parents have got unrealistic expectations for their kids," he says.

"Children need to build self-confidence," agrees John Alderson, who oversees the children's programs at Beaver Creek Resort in Colorado.

That means encouraging them to take lessons, especially when they are first learning. Ski experts explain that parents, no matter how adept, aren't trained to teach the sport, much less to lead children down the mountain in the games that improve their skills. Parents may not remember how difficult it was the first time they strapped those long skis onto their feet, encased in clunky boots. If your children are true beginners, consider a smaller ski resort. Not only will it be cheaper but children might find the place less intimidating.

Virtually all major ski resorts now offer children's ski school programming and even day care for babies. A growing number offer snow-boarding lessons as well. Steamboat Springs in Colorado offers kids free skiing much of the season. Vail now produces a special "Guide to Kids' Winter Vacations in the Vail Valley" (call Steamboat at 800-922-2722 and Vail at 800-4-SKI-KID). Children (and adults) with disabilities would have a wonderful time at Winter Park's Center for the Disabled (303-726-5514). Call 800-2-SKIWEE and ask where the respected children's ski program developed by *Ski Magazine* as well as the new "mini-rippers" snow-boarding program are being offered.

When you call a ski resort to book, see whether special family packages are available. Frequently, you'll save money if you book your entire trip from airfare to ski lifts through the ski area's central reservations number. Determine whether you need reservations for the kids' ski school or day care. Ask whether the children's instructors are specially trained to teach kids. Are the children divided by age as well as ability?

"Making the kids happy in the winter environment should be the parents' first goal," says Rick Devos, himself the father of two young children.

"The idea is for them to see the mountain as a big playground," agrees Dave Merriam, director of Stowe Mountain's Ski School in Vermont.

Younger children may be disoriented by the mountains and bustling ski school environment. They may not be used to so much snow or so many people. Don't let ski school be a child's first experience with day care, ski instructors ask. Start off slowly. If possible, show them around the ski school the day before they start.

---

1 🧳 Ski Gear

For all skiers in the family pack:

- Waterproof pants and jacket
- Warm waterproof mittens that stay on
- Warm hat (the longer and wilder, the better)
- Goggles
- Sunscreen (sticks are great)
- Long underwear
- Comfortable clothes that can be layered—turtlenecks, sweatpants, and sweatshirts work fine
- Heavy socks
- Neck gaiter
- Lip balm

Explain to younger ones that ski lessons will be a lot like preschool or day care. Tell the older ones how much fun they'll have exploring the mountain with a gang their own age. Buy them something they covet: cool goggles, a wild and crazy hat, a pin with the mountain insignia.

Even better, take them to a ski shop near home before the trip so they can try on skis and boots and get used to how they'll feel. Spread out a trail map on the table at home and talk about some of the runs you all hope to try together.

Remember, the more relaxed the children feel, the better they'll ski. If they're uptight, promise to check in during lunchtime. Show the kids the mountain's system to find parents, with notes posted on chalkboards at the top and bottom of every lift. Promise to ski with them at the end of the day to see what they've learned.

Parents who are paying more than fifty dollars a day per child to introduce their kids to the sport won't want to waste a minute. But a slow start—even permitting them not to ski when they choose—will pay off in the end. They might be tired or scared. They may just not be in the mood. They may have lost their nerve on a run that was tougher than they expected.

Better to quit early than risk a child deciding they never want to ski again. Let them spend the day playing in the snow or even inside. Some ski areas, Vail among them, now offer an indoor option for young skiers one day in the middle of the week.

The skiers in my family, meanwhile, never would consider a day off the slopes. I'm the only one who seems to need one.

23

Beach and Water Smarts

Grab the ice cream scooper, ruler, butter knife, and spray bottle. Don't forget the garden trowel or plastic strawberry boxes. Then head to the beach.

That's all you need to transform the beach lovers in your house into a team of sculptors who can produce wonderful creations: dragons, mermaids (the ice cream scoops make great hair), towers (use the strawberry boxes for bricks), and, of course, castles surrounded by moats.

Here's a tip from one prize-winning sand sculptor: Pack the sand down hard (suggest the kids jump up and down on it) and keep it as wet as possible. Start by building a sand volcano with water in the middle. The width should match the proposed height. Then carve from the top down.

Or try a dribble castle: Dribble wet sand out of your hand and build up a tower.

"It's much easier than it looks," says Thea Haubrich, a Virginia teacher who has led a team of youngsters to create a winning entry in one of the country's leading sand castle–building contests, the Neptune Festival in Virginia Beach, Virginia.

Sand sculpting certainly can become a great family hobby, something everyone will enjoy together, no matter what their ages. The sculptures can be as complex or as simple as the kids' enthusiasm and your energy allows. They can be life-size or miniature.

The longer you're out in the sun, the more important it becomes to protect yourselves from sunburn. Because sunscreens haven't been tested sufficiently on infants, doctors say, the best advice is not to use one but to keep young babies in the shade. Make sure they wear a wide-brimmed sun hat too. Children older than six months should use a sunscreen with a sun protection factor (SPF) of at least fifteen. Look for one that's water resistant and provides multihour protection.

Encourage kids, no matter what their ages, to wear baseball hats, sunglasses with ultraviolet protection, and clothes that are made from tightly woven cotton. Two new companies now offer hats and clothing for children made with lightweight fabrics that offer protection from the sun: Seattle-based Saolumbra (800-882-7860) and Arizona-based Frogskin (800-354-0203). Be forewarned that T-shirt cotton doesn't offer much protection from the sun.

And no matter how diligent you are, get the kids out of the sun every ninety minutes or so, and give them plenty to drink so they don't get dehydrated.

Don't turn your back on young kids around the water for even a minute—even in a wading pool. Too many children drown or are permanently disabled when parents look away to grab a towel, answer a phone, or glance at a newspaper headline.

Even if your kids are accomplished swimmers, make it a family rule that they must be supervised in the water. Doctors strongly recommend that they go "feet first, first time" when hitting the water so they don't end up diving into a too-shallow pond or pool. At a beach, swim in an area watched by a lifeguard.

Of course you don't want to be a nag—especially on vacation. But if you explain why you've established these safety rules, older kids will cooperate. They don't want to get hurt or find themselves in situations they can't handle either. And the younger ones will follow their older siblings' lead.

If the family is going boating or canoeing, make sure everyone is wearing Coast Guard–approved life jackets, no matter how much they complain.

The best protection is to teach the kids how to swim. The more confident they feel in the water, the less likely they are to panic. Once they can swim, though, don't overestimate their ability in the water. Make sure they always swim in pairs and enforce rest breaks every thirty minutes. "You don't realize how tired they can get just playing in the surf," one spokesperson for the U.S. Lifesaving Association explains. Coax them out of the water to build one of those sand creations.

2 🧳 Tidepools

Tidepools are made for kids. They're those small rocky pockets along the ocean that hold the saltwater in when the tide goes out.

Entire communities of sea life live here—sponges, snails, sea slugs, jellyfish, mussels, and even octopi. There is an amazing array of colors, shapes, and sizes: purple sea urchins, red starfish, green anemones.

If you can, go to an aquarium first so everyone will recognize what they're seeing. Then at low tide, head out. Fall and even early winter are good times. Exploring doesn't cost anything. Just wear sneakers or aqua socks, bring extra clothes (because the kids are bound to get wet), and a first-aid kit.

Just be gentle. Don't let the kids take the creatures home. And make sure they leave them just the way they found them.

24

Theme Park Etiquette

Don't pull Tigger's tail or kick Donald Duck's legs. Let them know you're waiting by tapping them on the shoulder or calling their names. And make sure to get those autograph books, pens, and cameras ready.

Whichever theme park you visit, you're bound to run into some of the big, fuzzy characters with the goofy grins—maybe even Goofy himself at Disney World. If you're determined to hug as many as you can, consider a character breakfast or dinner. Sure they're overpriced, but the kids will go home with lots of memories, photos, and autographs.

The toddlers in your crowd may not be as enamored of the creatures as the rest of you. In fact, don't be surprised if they're so frightened they start crying. Don't force a three-year-old to hug Mickey Mouse if she doesn't want to, even if it means you won't get that classic shot for the photo album. There's always next trip.

And another theme park. From California to Florida to Texas to Ohio, major theme parks and smaller local ones—more than four hundred across the country—are forever rolling out new attractions designed to thrill, entertain, and entice parents and children of all ages back for more. There are heart-stopping rides and entire parks within parks designed for the prekindergarten set.

And don't ever force kids—no matter what their ages—to go on a ride. They've got their reasons for holding back. Even if you've waited a half hour and they suddenly decide at the front of the line they can't do it, get out of line and try something else.

But don't insist on seeing every attraction and riding every ride. You'll make yourselves—and the kids—miserable. Small children as well as older ones may prefer riding their favorites four times as opposed to trying every different one.

Know your family's tolerance for lines. Kids invariably get hungry and thirsty and—the worst—have to go to the bathroom, in the middle of lines. Be prepared. One strategy: Alternate attractions with waits with those that require none.

---

3 🧳 *What Age for Disney?*

You'll see lots of babies at Disney World and Disneyland. But they're just along for the ride.

Even a toddler won't get much out of the place. Four to six is a good age to introduce a child to the Disney magic: They're old enough to be excited about everything, but not too old to be embarrassed by posing with Mickey Mouse.

It doesn't matter either if you don't make it to Disney World until the kids are teenagers. No one is ever too old for the experience—not even you.

Remember that it's impossible to please everyone all of the time, especially if the kids are different ages. Talk about how the family will do something one child wants to do and then head for another child's favorite ride. When that doesn't work, consider splitting up so each adult can take the kids to the things they most want to do. If your kids are the kind that wander, dress them all in the same brightly colored T-shirts or baseball caps. They'll be easier to spot in a crowd.

Give teens (and even responsible preteens) the freedom to explore on their own once they know the lay of the land. Do they know where to meet you and what time? Do they know

---

4 🧳 Happy Souvenir Hunting

Souvenir shopping with kids can be miserable. They may beg for things everywhere you go. They may insist that only the $29.95 number will do, when you're convinced it will be forgotten the next day. Even if you say no most times, chances are you'll go over budget. These basic rules will help:

- Set the shopping ground rules before leaving home. Let the kids know exactly how much they may spend. One family I know lets each child start each vacation day with three dollars worth of quarters. They lose a quarter each time they misbehave or fight. Whatever they've got left at the end of the day is theirs to spend on souvenirs.

- Bring back money or stamps from another country. Give each child an album or special box to house their collection.

- Don't spend hours searching for the perfect memento—especially with younger children. Pick something and then leave. If you don't want to buy anything, explain that today is a "looking day" and that you'll buy something tomorrow. Distract them by offering to get an ice cream or a treat.

the name and phone number of the hotel where you're staying? Do they know what to do if they get lost? Theme parks are a good enclosed place for preteens to show parents they can be responsible on their own.

You will spend more money on more ridiculous things than you would ever have believed: giant lollipops, mouse ears, baseball caps that say "Grumpy." That's OK. It's all part of the experience. To save a little money, stash some healthy snacks, water, and juice boxes in your backpack to avoid stopping at every food stand you see. Bring along sunscreen and some sweatshirts or jackets if you plan to stay into the evening.

- For any aged child, look for things that are different from home. Fourth-grade teacher Lynn Sperling, for example, brought back a bleached cow skull from the Southwest and cotton still on the plant from the South to show her Midwestern students. They loved them.
- If a visit to a historic site is on the itinerary, let the kids get a small replica of the Golden Gate Bridge, for example, or the White House. Look for a reproduction of a historic toy.
- Don't forget to save some money for a few special impulse buys too. They're always the best souvenirs.
- Let the kids start their own collections to remember their trips. They can buy a postcard at every stop, writing a few lines about what they did there, send a card home to themselves with a special vacation memory written on the back, or keep extra copies of the same card for use later in school and art projects.

When the kids have had enough—when everyone is tired, hungry, and cranky—it's time to leave, even if you haven't hit the star attraction. Go back to the hotel and go for a swim. Rest. Eat. You can always come back later or another day. The kids won't care if they see everything. And if it's a hot day, everyone will have a lot more fun splashing in a pool than waiting on a long line.

Cruise Smarts

Kids are everywhere on cruise ships these days, jumping in the swimming pools, lining up for ice cream cones, sunning themselves on deck, playing basketball for hours, jamming the video arcades, gobbling up sweets at the midnight buffets.

Families account for some five hundred thousand cruisers a year—nearly double what they numbered just a few years ago. Many are doting grandparents treating their grandchildren to a shipboard trip or inviting the entire family along for a reunion. "You've got to go with the grandchildren while you're feeling young enough to enjoy them and while they still want to go with you," says one Miami grandma.

Others are single parents who like cruises because they're certain to find other adults for companionship.

For many families, cruises offer an ideal vacation: The price is all-inclusive and plenty of activities exist to amuse every age group.

"Don't expect a lot of educational value. It's just fun," says Reva Denlow, a Chicagoan who has cruised several times through her four children's teen years. The ship, she says, provides just what her family needs: an opportunity to spend time together away from the stresses and strains of home, work, and school. For other families, a cruise ship offers a promise that parents will get a break too, while the kids are happily ensconced with new friends in organized activities from morning until night.

There's plenty for kids to do whether they're four or fourteen. "Cruises are fun because you don't have to be with your parents all the time and have good manners," says one young

5 Pint-sized Shutterbugs

Photography is an easy way to encourage children to take a closer look at the new places they're seeing on vacation. Hand kids a simple point-and-shoot or single-use camera and suggest they snap what makes them happy on the trip. Even a ten-year-old can shoot video as well with some supervision. Here are some tips from photography teachers for the shutterbugs in your family:

- Take outdoor pictures in morning or late afternoon on sunny days. Use natural light whenever possible.
- Remind the kids that you'll see what the camera sees; be careful not to chop off someone's head in the picture.
- Don't be afraid to move in close and try different angles.
- Concentrate on people. Don't neglect funny snapshots of the family dog or the kids clowning at the campsite—they're frequently the best.
- Have the kids create a story theme they can continue on the video throughout the entire trip. Ready, set, click!

veteran cruiser. Even preteens can have the run of the ship without parents being concerned about their safety. "My son could stay out as late as he liked and I know he's right there on the ship," explains one New York City widow.

Cruise lines, like resort hotels, are making increasing efforts to program for teenagers. There are teen discos, teen centers, and special shore excursions. Cruise officials work hard to keep teens out of bars and casinos—and out of trouble. The responsibility for their safety, though, rests with the parents.

Before booking, however, it's important to check carefully to be sure the ship will offer programming for your-age child the week you sail. You don't want to arrive with a three-year-old only to discover the activities start at age four or to board with a teenager and learn he's the only one on the ship. Is there a basketball court for the players in the family? Arts and crafts for your eight-year-old daughter? Plenty of water sports for everyone?

Typically, holiday and summer sailings on major ships are teeming with kids. Longer cruises to more exotic ports and luxury liners tend to have fewer families on board.

If you're looking for other cruising families, you should find plenty as long as you ask the right questions before you pay the deposit. Look for ships that tout their children's programs.

Virtually all cruises are booked through travel agents. Make sure yours has cruises with children or grandchildren or is familiar with all of the different children's programs.

The Family Cruise Club, a division of the Los Angeles–based Cruisemasters, is one good bet for booking a cruise for the family. Call 800-242-9000 for a "Parents Guide to Family Cruising." Also consider a major cruise discounter, like The Cruise Line Inc. at 800-777-0707. Take time to shop for the best deal.

Premier, Carnival, Norwegian, and Royal Caribbean are among the lines working hard to entice the family market with everything from Disney characters to the chance to sail with TV stars to special menus, movies, and even discos.

That's not to say the kids will want to spend every moment in some organized routine. And some families might find cruises too frenetic, with schedules too overloaded to be enjoyable. They might not like being surrounded by hundreds of strangers. Quarters are typically tight. And then there's seasickness. (Check with your doctor before sailing about seasickness remedies.)

But if you like plenty of action, a cruise might be for you. Though not exactly cheap, a cruise does give a family a lot of bang for a vacation buck because everything from meals to plane fare to accommodations and activities are included in the up-front price. There are few extras to pay for and no huge credit card bills to open the next month.

Even better, parents and older kids can go their own ways and meet for meals. There are no fights over where or what to eat for dinner or whether to hit the beach, the pool, or the video arcade.

"A lot of the decisions that cause stress are already made," explains one father.

26

National Parks

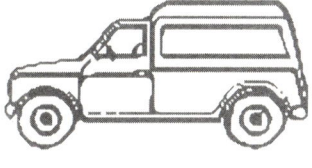

We have hiked to the top of a glacier and gawked at gushing waterfalls. We have scaled giant boulders, come face-to-face with a moose, made our way through a dense rain forest, and floated down the Colorado River. We have found all of these adventures and then some in the nation's national parks across the West.

There's no better place to introduce the kids to the outdoors. Programs galore exist, especially about animals, the first settlers, the mountains, and the desert.

Most of the nation's 367 national parks now offer junior ranger and other programs intended to make a visit more fun for kids and meaningful for their parents. They have ranger-led hikes and "discovery packs" kids can borrow to better explore the terrain, plus theatrical productions and campfires.

But the rangers complain that too many families who visit the national parks have the same problem: They're in too big a rush. "If they slowed down, they'd get much more out of the experience," suggests Allison Campbell, who oversees education programs at Muir Woods in northern California.

"We see a lot of exhausted kids and exasperated parents," agrees Candice Tinkler, Grand Canyon's education specialist.

That's not the way a visit to a national park should go. "We want kids to have a great experience," says Tinkler. "We want them to grow up understanding conservation and preservation and what the national parks are all about."

To get the most out of a park visit, plan ahead. You must make reservations at the most popular parks. Some places, like the Grand Canyon, Yellowstone, and Yosemite, are booked a year ahead for peak seasons. That's because people spend nearly as much time in the ten most popular parks than in all the rest combined.

The less-visited parks, though, offer just as many chances to hike, see wildlife, and camp and fish, with far fewer people. The ranger-led programs are just as good, and it's a lot easier to get a campsite or room nearby.

Consider North Cascades National Park north of Seattle, which has got heart-stopping mountain scenery and backcountry hiking but remains one of the least-visited parks in the country, while Washington State's Olympic National Park is one of the busiest.

If you plan to visit several parks in the next year, you can save money by buying a Golden Eagle Passport, available at all parks charging fees, for twenty-five dollars. It's good for a year and admits everyone in the same car.

Some parks, like Yellowstone and Glacier, are so vast it's important to earmark some of the places that are on the family's "must see" list. Special permits may be needed for certain activities, like backcountry camping. It's important to recognize that you can't see it all—even if you had a lifetime. Don't ruin your trip trying. Instead, take time to literally smell the flowers.

If you can, consider visiting during the off-season to avoid crowds. Many families, for example, love Yellowstone and Yosemite in winter. The Grand Canyon is just as awe-inspiring in September as in July—and a lot cooler.

If you've just got a weekend or an afternoon, consider spending it at a national historic site or a smaller park near your home. Work the hand looms at Lowell National Historical Park near Boston, Massachusetts, and see how the "mill girls" lived; or visit Ellis Island in New York where so many immigrants started their lives in the United States.

Many hands-on programs for families likely won't be promoted. "Families have to seek us out," concedes one park official. "We don't have a Disney World budget."

Wherever you are, ask the rangers how to make the most out of your visit. Which hikes are most appropriate for your-age

---

6 💼 Staking That Tent

Some of the most popular national parks offer reservations for campsites through MISTIX, a computerized reservation system. Sites can be booked up to eight weeks in advance. Call 800-365-CAMP.

Two other good resources for planning a national parks visit:

- *The Complete Guide to America's National Parks* from the National Parks Foundation.

- *Easy Access to National Parks* by Wendy Roth and Michael Tompane for The Sierra Club. It's an excellent guide for families with young children as well as for seniors and those with disabilities.

You can also call The National Park Service's Office of Public Inquires at 202-208-4747.

children? Where do you have the best chance to see wildlife? Are rangers leading any "scavenger hunts" in the woods for the kids the days you plan to visit? Any evening campfires? Chances are, you'll find more to do than at many resorts—certainly more than you'll have time for.

Hiking is one activity the whole family can enjoy. But don't expect the kids to react to the wilderness the way you do.

"Parents need to understand that a child's awe at an anthill is just as legitimate as a parent's awe at the top of the mountain," explains veteran hiker Maureen Keilty, who lives in Colorado and has written widely about hiking with children.

"When you're hiking with kids, you've got to let go of the idea of always getting to the top of the peak," explains Keilty, herself the mother of a young child. She recalled the group of Colorado children who stopped in their tracks on one trail to spend an hour watching an owlet learn to fly.

After several forays into the wilderness with Melanie, I've decided that the trick to hiking successfully with young children is to let them show you the world from their perspective. On one hike in Mount Rainier National Park, she stopped to turn

7 📖 Eco-Cool

Here are some ways rangers say families can help protect our national parks and other beautiful places:

- Brush your teeth using a minimum of water
- Pick up litter when you see it
- Turn off the lights whenever they're not being used
- Use rechargeable batteries
- Don't buy things with a lot of packaging
- Plant a tree in your yard

over every leaf, inspect every trickle from a mountain stream, and clamor up every rock, not to mention chatting with passers-by. Every minute or so, she would stray along the trail to inspect some new wonder.

You'll be amazed at what you discover together: tiny ladybugs, just-blossoming wildflowers, odd-shaped rocks.

Start the kids off small, with no more than a one-thousand-foot gain in altitude per mile. When the kids start complaining a lot, head back. You want a trail that's not too steep but offers plenty of variety. You also want one that leads to water of some kind—a waterfall, a lake. Check out the *Best Hikes with Children* series of thirteen books from the Mountaineers.

Teach the kids to stay on the trail and to stay put—"hugging a tree"—should they get separated from the rest of the group.

However far you're planning to hike, take lots of breaks. You don't want young ones to get hungry or thirsty either. So bring plenty of snacks, a water bottle for each hiker, and a few "surprise" treats when the troops insist they can't go another step.

Sturdy athletic shoes or hiking boots with well-padded socks are a must. So is a jacket, a hat, and sunscreen. Remember that weather can change rapidly. You don't want to be caught as we were halfway up the mountain without jackets when a hailstorm hit. Some extra lightweight pants are helpful too. On one hike, eight-year-old Reggie complained all the way back after she'd gotten soaked in a creek.

Even for a morning hike, a first-aid kit is also a must. Nothing is worse than a badly scraped elbow without a Band-Aid.

You don't have to carry everyone's gear, though. Even a three-year-old can carry a small day pack with her water bottle and windbreaker. Many kids like belly packs because they're easily accessible to keep "treasures" they've found (if it's permitted to take anything from the trail).

Try an "I found it!" scavenger hunt: When you leave the trailhead, hand each child a list of things they must find, along with a pencil to check off the list: a lizard doing push-ups, a condo for animals (a dead tree trunk). Whoever wins decides what's for dinner.

"Singing lots of songs helps too," says Stephanie Meismer, who grew up in Colorado and led her share of Girl Scout hikes there. Meismer's tip: Stock up on weird facts and legends about where you're hiking.

Stop at the park visitor center before heading out and pick up some pamphlets about animal tracks, plants, or Native American legends. On which hikes do the park rangers take their kids?

More than two hundred camps across the country now run family programs for part or all of the summer, where parents and kids alike participate in all kinds of camp activities, from swimming to arts and crafts to archery. You can have a gulp of Jello-red bug juice. Belt out "Row, Row, Row Your Boat" by the fire. Stage a shaving cream fight—against the kids.

Even better than the activities is the price, typically under $1,500 a week for a family of four. And no one has to cook dinner or wash dishes.

The YMCA runs family camps. So do university alumni associations from UCLA and the University of Michigan, among other places.

Call the American Camping Association at 800-428-2267 or check the library for the association's *Guide to Accredited Camps*.

Camping is an affordable way to visit the parks. No wonder so many '90s families are packing up sleeping bags, tents, and kids and heading out to sleep under the stars. But it can be one long bad dream for families not prepared to "rough it."

Don't worry if you're a neophyte. Today more products than ever are aimed at camping families, from kids' outdoor clothing to boots to family-sized tents. And with campsites typically under twenty dollars a night, it won't require nearly as much an investment as a couple of nights in a hotel, eating in restaurants. Your family may get more out of it than you expect.

Check to see if you'll need a camping reservation. Then make sure everyone—especially small children—know what they're in for. Practice setting up the tent in the backyard before you leave home. Give the kids a lesson in fire safety and what to do if they get lost in the woods. (Giving everyone a whistle to wear around their necks is always a good strategy.)

Even with all the advance planning, it likely won't turn out to be the perfect family experience you wanted. It probably will rain. The kids will whine that the tent is too small. Everyone will be too cold—or too hot. The mosquitoes will be fierce.

That's why the experts urge that you not blow a bundle on expensive gear until you've camped a few times. Make sure you like it. You'll know better then what you really need.

Just remember why you took the kids camping in the first place. Relax and forget about all the work waiting at home.

Don't forget the matches—or the sleeping bags.

27

Kids Abroad

They're touring the Louvre, snapping pictures from gondolas in Venice, and ogling the Crown Jewels in the Tower of London. The invasion of the newest tourists to hit the continent is going full force: American children, accompanied by their parents, have arrived.

There's no telling what an American child will get out of a trip abroad. But one thing's for sure: Touring overseas with a child will be an entirely different experience than you would have had otherwise. That's not necessarily bad—as long as you know that before boarding your flight.

You won't have hours to stare at one painting or to shop. You won't be able to linger over a four-course meal unless you arrange for a sitter or have children old enough to stay by themselves. But you will have the chance to explore an entirely new country together as a family. You may be the only people in a restaurant to speak English or react the same way to a statue.

You'll build memories that will last a lifetime and have a lot of adventures along the way. Sure the kids will get a lot out of a trip abroad—just not necessarily what you expect them to remember. "It's a different way to experience Europe, but adults can get a lot out of it too," says one mother who has traveled extensively abroad with her family.

Don't expect your four-year-old to spend hours touring French cathedrals or Italian museums. He or she will be a lot happier chasing pigeons and choosing pastries.

Likewise, your ten-year-old will pick different parts of the British Museum to see than you would have and will force you to learn a lot more history about those buried in Westminster Abbey.

No matter what their ages, kids will make friends wherever they go. Take advantage of that entrée. Spend time talking to other families and learning how they live. Don't worry about the language barrier. Kids will manage to communicate. "The kids bring you into the life there. We talked to the mothers and

---

8 *Books to Travel By*

First on my list would be Valerie Deutsch and Laura Sutherland's *Innocents Abroad, Traveling with Kids in Europe*.

Grade-schoolers heading to London or Paris might enjoy reading the *Kidding Around* series.

Look for children's books or videos set in the countries you'll be visiting:

- *Madeleine* in France
- *Heidi* in Switzerland
- *Hans Brinker and the Silver Skates* or *The Diary of Anne Frank* in the Netherlands

shopkeepers and old men. People strike up conversations because of the kids," says New Yorker Ruth Galen, who traveled through Italy with her toddler.

Plan your itinerary and then cut it in half. Don't try to make it to three countries in a week. Ask the kids what they want to see. Castles in Germany? Armor? Theater in London? Do they want to hike in Switzerland? Make it a family project to research the countries and what everyone wants most to see.

Make sure to build in plenty of free time once you get there just to absorb the atmosphere. Try staying in some smaller towns where everyone can get a feel for the culture and people of the country. Head to parks or beaches where the kids can meet other children their age. Allow younger ones to stick to their nap routines.

Try to avoid switching hotels every night, if you can. Younger children especially will find that difficult. Consider anchoring your trip at a cottage, condo, or villa and exploring just one region. "It was so relaxing," recalls one mother of two young children who did just that in Italy.

Let the kids shop in local markets for picnics. Encourage them to try new foods. You may be amazed what they're willing to try in a new environment.

One seventh grader, a picky eater at home, dared try sautéed sea slugs, jellyfish, and chicken feet during a week in China with his parents on a business trip.

"I amazed myself," he says. "But the Chinese eat those things all of the time and I wanted to try them."

No matter how exotic or beautiful the locale, remember that your kids, after all, are still just kids. They'll whine. Siblings will argue. They'll complain about being in the car too long.

And they'll pick a playground any day over a cathedral. Wouldn't you?

28

Pass the Culture, Please

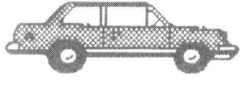

The roomful of artists at the Art Institute of Chicago concentrated intently on the project at hand—making miniature rooms, shaping their creations carefully out of bits of paper, fabric, and pictures cut from glossy art catalogs, with gentle suggestions from the workshop instructors.

Some of these artists weren't even in kindergarten yet. Others were past retirement.

"This is as much fun for me as for the kids," laughed Linda Dawe, a speech pathologist from suburban Chicago who was "creating" alongside her kids.

"When we say we're coming downtown, the girls want to come here," continued Dawe. "Definitely, they think the art museum is a fun place."

That's precisely the point, of course. Whether it's the Art Institute of Chicago; the Metropolitan Museum of Art in New

York; the Museum of Fine Arts, Boston; the J. Paul Getty Museum in California; Washington D.C.'s National Gallery of Art; or one of the smaller regional art centers such as Santa Fe's Museum of Indian Arts and Culture, major art museums around the country are working hard to get the same message across to families: We've got plenty for you, just give us a try.

And, reports the American Symphony Orchestra League, from Yakima to Los Angeles and Omaha to New York, hundreds of large and small orchestras around the country are working toward that same goal with more programming for children.

At a time when schools are cutting back on music and art classes, orchestras, like museums, are stepping into the breach. They are offering more short concerts and inviting children to come before performances to meet the musicians or try some of the instruments. They are hoping, of course, to build the next

9 City Lights

Maybe the kids want to check out the tall buildings. Maybe they want to see what the street vendors have to offer. Maybe they just want to run around the park.

Face it. Sometimes it's more fun outside the museum or concert hall than inside.

And that's okay. Don't fret if you missed the end of the concert or half of the major exhibit. It's more important to give kids plenty of breathing room in between injections of culture and everyone will be a lot happier. You can slip in a lesson about the city you're visiting just by strolling down the main thoroughfares near museums and concert halls.

Do people look different than at home. Is the food different? Do kids talk differently here? Let your kids lead the way.

generation of concertgoers in the process. Tickets can be cheaper than a movie, $5 a person in some places.

"We've had to go back to the drawing board and redesign programming with a view that this is a child's first and, in too many cases, their only experience with classical music," says Jim Ruggirello, the Los Angeles Philharmonic's education director.

This at a time when parents are actively searching for ways to enrich their children's educations—and finding new activities to share. "I see the museum on a totally different level now and it's more fun," acknowledges Mary Beth Dermody, who also frequents Chicago's Art Institute workshop with her daughter. "We come all of the time now."

The trick, museum and music educators say, is to make the experience fun. Vacation times in a new city, when a family is searching for different activities from home, can be a first-rate opportunity for trying something like a classical concert or an art museum.

The kids might even like seeing the great historic buildings that house art museums and orchestra halls. Call to see what programs are available for children.

But whether it's a world-class art museum or a first-rate orchestra, don't try to force-feed culture to the kids. If there isn't a concert specifically geared for youngsters, try an open rehearsal or outdoor arts festival.

"You've got to find something they can relate to so that it has power in their lives," adds B. J. Adler, who administers arts programs around the country for families.

Plan your visit to the museum or orchestra hall. Which galleries will you see? Pick a theme like faces or nature. Can your children imagine stepping inside a painting?

Composing a symphony? See what the kids can find out about the composer's life. Have them listen to the music beforehand so it will seem familiar. Visit a music store so they can see the instruments up close. "It's a success if the kids leave wanting to come back for more," says Polly Kahn, education director for the New York Philharmonic.

Stop at the museum shop on your way into the museum and buy a couple of postcards of famous works of art. Turn the visit into a bonafide treasure hunt. Some museums have institutionalized that practice.

Bring a sketchbook and let the kids draw their own versions of the masterpieces they see.

Museums, meanwhile, have plenty to choose from to engage the kids' interest—art classes, performances, and special family guides to exhibitions and galleries. The Museum of Indian Arts and Culture in Santa Fe, for example, enables youngsters to explore Native American culture by trying their hand at crafts like pottery or weaving. There even are videos and games to do at home, along with a growing library of books for children about art and artists.

Even disinterested young museum and concertgoers—like my eleven-year-old son, Matt—might be surprised by what they find inside a museum or orchestra hall these days.

"It was O.K." Matt admitted after one recent visit. Some days, that's as good as you'll get.

29

Adventures to Go

Paul hiked up an Alaskan glacier, kayaked in the rain alongside whales and sea lions, and saw bald eagles and bears—all before he was three.

"It's such a wonderful experience, who else would you want to share it with besides your kids," asks Paul's mom, an attorney from West Los Angeles. "I would hate to leave the kids behind."

Across the country in Greenwich, Connecticut, the normally sedentary Scharff family is still raving about the horsepack trip they took in the Arizona mountains. "It was so different from the pressures of our daily lives," explains Louise Scharff, a Manhattan magazine editor who, along with her husband and 10- and 13-year-old sons, rates the rugged camping trip "right up there with Disney World."

"We want to do it again," she says—this despite a miserable spill off a horse into an icy stream and a hailstorm. "It was a big adventure that we could have together," she laughs.

At roughly $2,000 to $2,500 (excluding air) for a family of four, these adventures won't cost any more than Disney World.

Some trips are considerably cheaper. It's no wonder that so many outfitters are working hard to tailor trips for these eager families, sending them canoeing in the Minnesota Boundary Waters Canoe Area, kayaking in Mexico, snorkeling in Hawaii, llama trekking in New Mexico, white-water rafting in Colorado, biking in California, and hiking in Maine.

"We don't want to lose our youth," laughs Dede Pahl, a Denver administrator of a nonprofit agency. "It's denial all the way," she jokes, noting that her family—including her husband, teenaged son and preteen daughter—had "the best fun we ever had" on a white-water rafting trip last summer. "We go in a million different directions at home," she said. "This trip really gave us the opportunity to connect as a family . . . while the kids still want to take trips with us."

Just remember that the kids won't react to the adventure or the wilderness the same way you might. They might get scared.

They might get bored.

That's why it's important to choose an outfitter that is experienced with children. It's also important to choose a trip where there will be other kids, as well as plenty of opportunities for them to succeed at whatever they try. It needn't be that exotic to qualify as an adventure—just decidedly different from what they do at home.

Other payoffs to adventures include spending unstructured time together exploring and gaining an understanding of the wonders of the outdoors. There's something really wonderful about watching your kids experiment with the new—the triumphant look when they get it right, their discovery that they really don't need television or video games to amuse themselves, their learning that patience does get rewarded . . . sometimes at least.

Take fishing. On her first try, Reggie cast her brand-new Snoopy fishing pole so hard that the little yellow rod and reel went right over the side of the boat into the deep, blue Minnesota lake.

Reggie looked stricken. Her brother guffawed. Luckily, Dad came to the rescue, snaring the pole with his net just as it was about to sink and Reggie to burst into tears. Good thing, too. On her very next cast, she caught a largemouth bass big enough

---

10 📖 Pedal Pushers

Name one thing everyone in the family can do together, at home or on vacation, that's healthy, environmentally friendly, and even free.

Dust off those bikes and join the 100 million Americans who are taking their kids and heading to bikepaths and backroads. Growing numbers of companies now offer family-friendly bike tours. (To start on your research, call the League of American Bicyclists at 800/288-BIKE and order The Tourfinder, a complete listing of bicycle touring companies, for seven dollars.)

You can bike in national parks, through rolling farmland, around lakes, or near the ocean.

Just be realistic about how far the kids can pedal, typically no more than five to ten miles a day. Plan the route in advance—even driving it, if possible. Wear comfortable clothes and be sure to bring plenty of snacks. Baby powder helps protect backsides as well as feet.

To protect everyone's heads, bike helmets—even for the youngest in the group—are key. Don't bike without them.

for dinner. "Wow!" was all a flabbergasted Reggie could muster. Just six at the time, she's been hooked on fishing ever since.

Her brother, Matt, meanwhile, has loved to fish since before he went to kindergarten. It didn't matter that he caught few "keepers" then: reeling in the bluegills from the edge of the dock, throwing them back, and watching them swim off was thrill enough. I spent much of that trip to Minnesota threading slimy worms on Matt's hook—true motherly devotion, I've always thought.

Now Matt and Reggie have their own tackleboxes and earnestly discuss the merits of various lures, hooks, and bait with their dad, leaving me totally out of the loop on this one.

The "lucky" Snoopy pole belongs to Melanie, who is still happy to have Mom bait her hooks.

30

Cows and Ducks and Horses

The middle-aged suburban mother's idea of a vacation is sitting by the pool with a good book—certainly not bumping up and down on a horse all day in the wind and rain.

"I know what it's like to be around smelly animals," explains the forty-four-year-old woman. "I grew up on a farm."

But she gamely went along to a Colorado dude ranch with her husband, an airline pilot, and two kids. "I didn't equate ranching with fun."

She couldn't have been more wrong. "I had the time of my life. It was the best family vacation we ever had," she said.

Dude ranches have been around for nearly a century, starting when adventurous Easterners asked for a chance to experience life on a Western cattle ranch. They didn't want to accept the hospitality free, though, and asked the ranchers to charge, explains the Dude Ranchers' Association, which now numbers more than 100 members.

Those first guests paid just ten dollars a week for the privilege of riding and relaxing far away from their homes. Today's visitors spend nearly ten times that. But ranching has never been more popular, as growing numbers of families discover it provides an ideal antidote to the pressures of urban and suburban life and teaches kids about the outdoors in the process.

Other families are heading to farms around the country for the same reason, trying to give city kids the chance to milk cows, gather eggs from the henhouse, or watch in wonder as kittens are born. "It's just nice and easygoing, totally different from home," one suburban mother explains. Her five-year-old spent the week gathering eggs and chasing newts while her niece camped at the bunny hutch. The place was small enough to afford even younger kids an element of freedom. For one family, just the idea of not going into an elevator to go outside was exciting.

Like ranches, some farms have organized children's programs while others provide little more than a room and bath in the midst of a family farm, enabling parents and kids to jump in and help as they like.

For a list of farmers who take in guests, call the tourism departments in farming states such as Vermont, Pennsylvania, Iowa, and Wisconsin. Then, whether you're heading for a Western ranch or an East Coast farm, ask ahead what is planned for the youngsters. Is there programming for the children your kids' ages? Are there baby-sitters?

Remember that ranches typically are small, hosting fewer than fifty guests, and they're not all alike. That's why it's important to make sure the one you pick has what your family needs. Call and talk to the ranch owner yourself. Ask how old the children must be to ride (most programs start at age six). If you've got younger kids, see what activities are provided for them. Do guests stay in cabins or single rooms?—an important consideration if you're arriving with a couple of kids.

Do children eat with their parents or separately with counselors? Are sitters available for the baby? What else is there for the kids to do? Most ranches offer fishing, rafting, swimming, hiking, nature lessons, sightseeing, and, at some places, tennis and gourmet meals.

Single parents find the joint activities and meals make ranches and farms a good choice for their families, while grandparents suggest they're good spots for family reunions. Stephanie Slade, herself the mother of four, teaches the kids riding at Tanque Verde Guest Ranch in Arizona, which has been a ranch for more than a century and a guest ranch since the 1950s. Her tip: Make sure the kids come with shoes or boots with heels. Don't forget sunscreen and hats either.

"Being with an animal like this is an experience you just don't get in L.A. or Philadelphia," observes Slade. That's clearly one for the kids' memory book. Yours too.

For a five dollar national directory of ranches, call the Dude Ranchers' Association at 303–223–8440. A directory of more than forty Colorado Ranches is available free from Colorado Dude and Guest Ranch Association. Call 303–887–3128.

Epilogue

Happy Travels

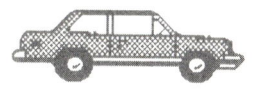

The old snapshots had been tossed in the bottom of a box, piled helter-skelter in no particular order. There were the kids mugging for the camera on skis, posing with Minnie Mouse, triumphantly holding up a just-caught fish, and standing atop a mountain trail after a rigorous hike.

I found the photos as I was unpacking after a recent cross-country move. Some I hadn't seen in years. They made me stop in the midst of an all-too hectic day and smile, savoring the memories of those long-past vacations.

Suddenly I was back on a Florida beach with my much-younger trio, building sand castles and chasing waves. I could feel the warm sunshine even as I remembered the frustration of tagging after an ever-curious toddler.

Soon I started thinking about trips I took as a child—one to Washington, D.C.; another to a lake. It didn't matter where we went so much as the happy feelings those times together evoked.

Other parents and grandparents have echoed my feelings. Even if it's necessary to stretch the budget to make the trip, families agree that the time together is worth it. On vacation, it seems, there's time to get to know the grandchildren or stepdaughter better. There's time to figure out what that thirteen-year-old is really thinking and why the nine-year-old loves soccer so much. There's time to turn the tables, for parents to act goofy and for kids to act grown-up.

Family trips also offer the opportunity for everyone to stretch a little, to see new places, try new foods, and meet families different from their own. Perhaps you and the kids will discover a new sport together, one that you might share for the rest of your lives.

That's why I don't think family vacations should be considered an "extra" to be undertaken only in good times. Frankly, I think they're necessary to help our families keep going.

In fact, we may need the break they provide even more when things aren't going well. I don't mean scraping the bottom of the bank account, of course. I just mean penciling in some time with the kids away from home.

The payoff will come years from now, when everyone relives those times again and again—over Thanksgiving dinner, at weddings, and at funerals too.

Don't let me paint too rosy a picture, though. None will be perfect. As I was flipping through our old photos, the hassles and aggravations of all those trips came flooding back too, including the lost luggage in the Caribbean, the terrible bout of flu in California, the backseat battles in Minnesota, the family spat at the reunion, the long theme-park lines. These trials and tribulations nearly wrecked our plans—and our spirits—but in retrospect, they seemed a small price to pay for the wonderful experiences we've shared, and, of course, the memories. Now, the kids like to play the "remember when we went to . . . " game as much as we do.

Sure family vacations are a lot of work, especially, it seems, for mothers. All of the planning. All of the packing and unpacking, not to mention the laundry. And all of that expense. Invariably, everything costs more than the budget calls for.

But I'm convinced that such trips, whether to a small cabin at a nearby lake or to an exotic foreign city, are always worth the trouble and the money. It's time and dollars well-spent. Consider family vacations an investment—in the family and in the future. Go somewhere close to home if you can't afford to fly. Go for a weekend instead of a week. But go before it's too late, before the kids are grown and gone.

That way, when things get rocky—and they always do from time to time—you can pull out the old photos and the memories along with them. Thinking about past vacations helps us and the kids through any rough spots. Those trips also help us to focus again on what really matters in our lives. Most important, they force us to stop, if only for a short while, to consider all the happy things going on in our lives.

Just remember the secret to a successful trip with the kids: It won't be perfect. Tell yourself that at least six times a day. Believe it and you'll do fine. You might even find yourself laughing instead of yelling when everything goes wrong at once.

That's what I do. It works every time.

Have you got any funny family travel stories? Send them to Taking the Kids, 578 Post Road East, Westport, CT 06880. They may be used in my column.